MW01713585

Praise For "Employee Performance Scorecards"

Employee Performance Scorecards is an exceptional case study of how to create management discipline. It presents a specific, practical, and useful story that demonstrates the value of measures and accountability. Those interested in improving employee performance will find great value in the case study.

— Dave Ulrich
Professor, Ross School of Business, University of Michigan
Partner, The RBLGroup

When it comes to evaluating employee performance, Les Dakens gets it right. Unions and workers are always suspicious of any evaluation scheme. If employers followed all the steps of the *Employee Performance Scorecards*, I see nothing but positive outcomes. Workers need to know that their contributions are recognized and valued.

— Bryan Neath
Assistant to the National President
UFCW Canada
(United Food & Commercial Workers Canada)

Why in most companies do we exclude unionized employees from receiving the benefits of a performance evaluation? *Employee Performance Scorecards* tells the real story of how one company bucked this tradition and achieved positive results for everyone involved. This is a wonderful guide to any company who aspires to this level of effective people management. Let's all get on with the lessons *EPS* can teach.

— Helen Handfield-Jones, Co-Author of the book *War on Talent*

This book is very inspirational for leaders who want to do the right thing! Often unions are considered to be a roadblock. However, with the right partnership and management attitude, they can assist you in achieving your objectives.

— Renée Légaré

Senior Vice President, Human Resources

Canadian Air Transport Security Authority Administration

Employee Performance Scorecards describes a creative and powerful approach to demonstrate the linkage of employee contribution to driving value to the top and bottom lines. While *EPS* might be confused with a traditional dashboard, it is so much more. This quick read will enlighten anyone interested in enabling a performance culture in their organization.

This book is very inspirational for leaders who want to do the right thing! Often unions are considered to be a roadblock. However, with the right partnership and management attitude, they can assist you in achieving your objectives.

— Steve Berger

Senior Vice President, Human Resources and Transformation

Viterra

This book provides a great example of how companies should lead versus direct their employees, to make them feel more engaged and part of a team. This definitely results in greater productivity and employee satisfaction. The Book also shows that a union will support these programs as long as they understand what the company is trying to accomplish. I enjoyed reading the story about *Employee Performance Scorecards*.

— Buzz Hargrove

(Retired) President

Canadian Auto Workers Union

Employee Performance Scorecards is a basic tool that so many companies struggle with. It was inspiring to read about an HR team that had the motivation to do what they knew was the best thing for the company. As Les wrote, there were no barriers, only hurdles; hurdles that the HR team managed to get around.

I believe that many of us do not realize the power of performance feedback. Not only can it change an organization, it directly impacts the bottom line. *EPS* is a "must read" for those who want to make that impact!

— Diane Nyisztor

Vice-President, Corporate Human Resources, SNC-Lavalin Group Inc.

When I first read the manuscript of *Employee Performance Scorecards* I was so excited. I quickly sent off emails to my colleagues saying this book is a must read. It tells you all the "how to" steps of implementing a Performance Management process with a large, diverse, unionized workforce and does so in a clear, practical and doable way. This book provides insights into how Performance Management can be a catalyst for helping to unleash the raw energy and talents in a unionized environment. A superb "hands-on" guide.

— Jim Grossett

Senior Vice President, Human Resources,

Agrium Inc.

Practical, informative and useful — Les Dakens provides the how-to and how-not-to guide to enhancing performance in a unionized environment. *Employee Performance Scorecards* shows that traditional barriers to employee review can be managed effectively to create a win-win for both management and unions.

— Richard C. Powers
Associate Dean and Executive Director
MBA and Master of Finance Programs
Joseph L. Rotman School of Management
University of Toronto

Employee Performance Scorecards is an excellent companion book to Switchpoints. It demonstrates how a feedback tool and the process associated with it can support change management and drive the right behaviors throughout the organization. The book reminds us that many supervisors are not leaders and that many do not know the people who report to them. It underscores the virtues of feedback and the desire of just about all employees to do the right thing. This provides supervisors a greater opportunity to leverage the skills of their people. Lastly we are reminded that communication is vital for an organization to reach its potential.

— Andrew K Mittag
President
Agrium Advanced Technologies

I found the book an interesting and entertaining read. Clearly a vision and a strong desire to achieve propelled a team of dedicated professionals to implement a significant change within the organisation. The challenges of designing the EPS system, influencing the operational managers to support it, and then successfully deploying it across 18,000 unionized employees, in an industry where this is not the norm, is a testament of strong leadership and dedication. I also believe that linking the motivation to implement *EPS* to the bottom line of the company was a fundamental ingredient that made the project a success. From my experience as a manager, truly engaging the people that support that bottom line, can only lead to success; congratulations on your achievement.

— Cesar Inostroza

Vice President & General Manager

Aluminum Division

SNC-Lavalin Inc.

Regardless of your function or industry, *EPS* is the gold standard and a must read if you are interested in how behavior of an employee can be changed and the culture of an organization transformed.

— Martin J. Parker

Managing Director

Waterstone Human Capital Ltd.

Thought Leadership Series

EMPLOYEE PERFORMANCE SCORECARDS

CREATING A WIN-WIN FORMULA FOR YOUR ORGANIZATION

LES DAKENS

CARSWELL®

© 2009 Thomson Reuters Canada Limited

NOTICE AND DISCLAIMER: All rights reserved. No part of this publication may be reproduced, stored in a retrieval system, or transmitted, in any form or by any means, electronic, mechanical, photocopying, recording or otherwise, without the prior written consent of the publisher (Carswell).

Carswell and all persons involved in the preparation and sale of this publication disclaim any warranty as to accuracy or currency of the publication. This publication is provided on the understanding and basis that none of Carswell, the author/s or other persons involved in the creation of this publication shall be responsible for the accuracy or currency of the contents, or for the results of any action taken on the basis of the information contained in this publication, or for any errors or omissions contained herein.

No one involved in this publication is attempting herein to render legal, accounting, or other professional advice. If legal advice or other expert assistance is required, the services of a competent professional should be sought. The analysis contained herein should in no way be construed as being either official or unofficial policy of any governmental body.

A cataloguing record for this publication is available from Library and Archives Canada.

ISBN 0-978-7798-2261-4

THOMSON REUTERS

CARSWELL, A DIVISION OF THOMSON REUTERS CANADA LIMITED

One Corporate Plaza
2075 Kennedy Road
Toronto, Ontario
M1T 3V4

Customer Relations
Toronto 1-416-609-3800
Elsewhere in Canada/U.S. 1-800-387-5164
Fax 1-416-298-5082
www.carswell.com
E-mail www.carswell.com/email

About the Author

Les Dakens was the former Senior Vice-President, People, for CN. Previously, he was the North American Vice-President of Human Resources with the HJ Heinz Company. He held leading HR roles for Cadbury Beverages, and started his career with Nortel. He has had experience with many of the largest unions in Canada and the U.S, including the CAW, the Teamsters, the United Steelworkers, the United Electrical Workers, and the United Food and Commercial Workers.

Les is the co-author of the successful business book Switchpoints: Culture Change on the Fast Track to Business Success, published in 2008. Currently, he runs Pineridge Consulting Inc., a firm specializing in coaching for executives.

All of the author's proceeds from the EPS book will be donated to the Alzheimer Society of Canada, to support their research efforts.

This book is dedicated to Peter, who made it happen.

Table of Contents

PREFACE

Employee Performance Scorecards is a true story about a ground-breaking change in the workplace. The story involved taking an unusual stance: including every employee in the performance management system. Such inclusions are not the norm in organizations that are unionized. In most such companies, only non-unionized employees participate in performance evaluations.

There are many reasons why unionized employees are not included in the performance management system. The most likely answer is that it is not traditional to include them. What has been done in the past often has a powerful hold over the vision and imagination of people, and they stay within its confines. If reviews haven't been done in the past, few managers will ask "Why not?"

Or the answer could be that management is uncertain of what benefit there would be in giving unionized employees performance feedback. At the best of times, managers are uncertain of the benefits of performance reviews. Many managers avoid doing them at all, and many more do them poorly.

Another source of uncertainty is how some managers see unionized employees. Typically, managers perceive that such employees owe their primary allegiance to a union, rather than to the company that employs them. Accordingly, those employees get exactly what is spelled out in a collective agreement, but nothing else, because they're on the "other side".

A further response could be that doing reviews with unionized employees might cause trouble with the unions. "Don't go looking for trouble, it has your address," and "Don't upset the apple cart," are maxims deeply carved into some managers' brains. When "don't" is the imperative behind managers' thinking, there is no incentive to think outside of the customary box.

Lurking behind any answer is likely some fear of change. There have been dramatic changes over the last two decades, and people are growing weary of it. It probably isn't going to stop any time soon, and the old status quo is gone for good. A different status quo may take hold when the pace of change drops, and if companies want to be positioned well for it, they need to be proactive.

The key to success in the future is likely to be similar to the one that dominates now. A relevant product or service, at the right price and well differentiated against the competition is the opening gambit, backed up by disciplined management practices and engaged employees at all levels. It's a fairly precise description, but there are no simple formulas to achieve success.

Successful leaders typically place heavy emphasis on growth in business performance, at least partially achieved through growth in individual performance. Very few people are likely to achieve that growth without feedback and differentiated information on their work performance. Accordingly, performance reviews, despite wide disdain for them among the management ranks, are a vital, basic tool in achieving business success.

Perhaps some of North America's heavily unionized companies would be in a better position right now if their leadership had paid attention to the basics in managing people. Productivity is quite often the first thing to decline when employees lack engagement in their work. Ideas about how to improve processes, information on customers' needs and suggestions about business opportunities decline as well.

Industries once at the heart of North America's prosperity — steel, pulp and paper and automotive — are all in decline. Yet, these industries thrive elsewhere, so the products are needed. Maybe the problem is the way these companies have been run. Perhaps they were all once convinced of their invincibility, and brought low by their inability to adapt over time to stay relevant and competitive.

Their perennial defense is the cost of their union contracts, and the burden it places on their profitability and revenue. The quick answer is that companies get the unions that they deserve. People who are engaged in their work and energized by it, and who feel that they are treated fairly, are rarely the ones who make unreasonable demands for rewards. Job satisfaction has multiple components, but perhaps if monetary rewards are the only ones open to you, maybe that's the route you take.

Performance reviews don't have to be complicated to be effective. They are not a panacea for business troubles, but they are a simple way to have direct conversations with every employee and open up two-way communication. They are certainly, for most employees, the first step toward engagement.

In companies where a large percentage of the total employee headcount is unionized, it is more, not less, important to work hard at engaging employees. It is only when they are engaged that they make contributions that go beyond their job descriptions. It is at that point where people move from compliance — doing the job to earn a salary — to being committed to the organization's success and being willing to do what it takes to make it happen.

Companies and their unions want businesses to be successful. While their definitions of success may vary to some degree, they are definitely in it together. So maybe the challenge is for organizations to treat every employee the same way, whether they are unionized or not. It goes back to the old saying: "You have to give, to get." If what you are giving is the opportunity for employee engagement, what you are likely to get is better performance.

ACKNOWLEDGEMENTS

It is my good fortune to have worked with many talented HR and LR colleagues, and I have learned a great deal from them. Seeing them in action on the EPS project was a joy to watch, for it was their hard work, dedication and openness that made it work. With very few exceptions, they took ownership over it, and they were the ones who brought it across the finish line. Other colleagues were equally supportive and involved. Thank you, everyone, who believed in the project.

Judy Johnson and George Greanis from CLG (Continuous Learning Group) provided good support to the project, and worked hard to help make it happen (their ABC, DCOM and Q4 Models were invalvable). A number of union leaders, who prefer to remain anonymous, offered useful feedback and encouragement.

I have also had the good luck to work with great business minds. They could plainly see that good business results depend upon people being helped to perform well, and that the two are always interconnected. To them, making sure that people were treated appropriately was taking care of business.

Thank you to Sheila and Ben at Carswell for believing in this story and making it come alive for the readers.

Finally, a big thank you to my wife Marijane. Without her direct assistance, this book would never have been completed.

THE PRELUDE

"I tell my people you don't have to go on strike to bring the company to its knees. All you have to do is stop taking initiative. Let your supervisors make all the decisions. Let them solve all the problems. Just do exactly what you're told."

A union leader

"It's all about people, folks. When you unleash the power of people, it's amazing what you can do."

The CEO of the company

CHAPTER 1

THE DREAM

It all started innocently enough. In preparation for the analysts' meeting in New York City in November 2005, the CEO of the company, part of the transportation industry, asked for a presentation from HR. He wanted to let the analysts know how much work the HR function had done around developing managers. That work was important, as it had provided a platform for the company's continuously improving bottom-line, which was always of interest to the analysts.

As the presentation got closer, the Senior Vice President of HR tried to imagine how the analysts would respond to all of the HR initiatives at the company, and sorted out which ones to include. The words "Earnings Per Share" kept running through his mind as he knew that the analysts used this key measure to evaluate and rate companies. There was something in the phrase that intrigued him, but he couldn't quite put his finger on it.

The phrase stayed with him, and triggered a long held idea. The company was the fourth organization where he had worked that had a significant union presence. None of these companies did performance evaluations with unionized employees. No one ever thought about it, because it just wasn't done. There was no mandate in the collective agreement to do it, and it wasn't on the management agenda. Those absent reviews were a missed opportunity.

And so the dream of Employee Performance Scorecards — EPS — was born.

Check Your Brains at the Door

Most large, unionized companies have something in common — there is a tendency on the part of managers not to treat unionized people as regular employees. Managers expect the unionized ranks to do what they are told, when they are told, but not to contribute their ideas. It's as though the unionized employees are supposed to check their brains at the door.

This behavior doesn't make any sense. Without unionized employees, and the myriad of jobs they do, none of these companies would have a business. Yet, out of 22,500 employees at the company, only 4,500 annual performance appraisals were done. A quick check of the arithmetic showed that meant 18,000 people didn't get a review, which left 80 per cent of the work force with no information on their performance.

The ones missing performance information were the unionized employees. Traditionally, the company did not do performance reviews with unionized workers. Why not include everyone? The short answer, that no performance reviews were done because the employees were unionized, was not good enough. If "tradition", used in the sense of "this is the way we've always done it" was the answer, then tradition was getting in the way.

The Distance Factor

To some extent, having a unionized work force is almost like outsourcing your employees. They work for the company, but the intermediary, the union, is the one that negotiates work conditions, pay and benefits through the collective agreement.

All interventions with unionized employees must be done with respect to this agreement, which creates a sense of distance between managers and employees.

The collective agreement is a piece of paper that tends to make managers nervous. Make a misstep with it, and serious trouble may result. There's a lot riding on keeping the peace. Keeping the peace is very different than helping everyone bring out their best. It also meant that supervisors didn't get to know their employees very well. They often were not aware of their employees' full work experience, or what they thought about the business or where they wanted to go in their careers.

The distance between supervisors and unionized employees did not work to anyone's advantage. Most people want to do a good job. Certainly, there are people who do not perform well. Any number of reasons can account for that poor performance, but very rarely is the reason a lack of desire on employees' part to be successful. It doesn't matter if someone is in the union or sitting in the corner office: a desire to be successful at what you put your hand to is part of the human condition.

It would be ground-breaking to let all employees know how their performance was seen by management. Without that performance information, there can be a real, yet invisible, barrier to success for people in doing their jobs as well as possible. With feedback, and an understanding of how their performance was seen, they would have a chance to leverage their strengths or work on areas of improvement. It would be their choice. Taking away that barrier would be the right thing to do.

Culture Change

The culture within the company had been undergoing change since the organization went public. Previously, making a profit was not at the top of the priority list. A job with the company meant life-long security. If you did your job well, that was fine, and if you didn't do it well, that was fine too. Managers and supervisors often avoided confronting unionized employees to the point where they had ceded control to them informally. In this atmosphere of abdication, productivity was low, customer service was abysmal and the safety record was spotty.

After the IPO, there was a change in the thinking of the company's management team. Profitability, to attract shareholders, became the watchword. Managers were encouraged to embrace a "command-and-control" approach to business, and sharp eyes focused on costs and productivity. Like all organizations that try to recreate themselves, these changes resulted in pain and distress for employees. It also meant opportunity, although it wasn't always easy for people to see it among the uncertainty, turmoil and job loss that accompanied the turnaround.

Some of that opportunity, of course, involved unionized employees. And in a new organizational climate, one that emphasized achievement, good employees began to get noticed.

Hidden Gems

The company had always had good employees. It was just that in the past being a good employee didn't get much notice. That lack of care hurt the employees a lot more than it helped them.

It is a huge disadvantage to people to be part of an organization that doesn't focus on making every employee successful.

Yet, because the company had good people, there were exceptions.

The Power of Ideas

Jim Moore, a transport driver and a long term employee, illustrates the power of ideas. He developed the idea that shutting down his engine when a product was being loaded from customers at plant and warehouse gates, would be worthwhile. Accordingly, Jim initiated this practice.

Some of his fellow drivers thought he was crazy. What did it matter? Everyone let their engines run. It was the way things were done. What difference would it make?

His actions made a big difference. In one year, his initiative saved about 500 gallons of fuel. While it represented a small amount of money in a large company, his actions demonstrated that employees on the line could have control of costs, and they could manage company assets well. It also meant that all those gallons of unburned fuel weren't adding any emissions to the air, which was a terrific bonus.

And that was only one truck. There were hundreds of trucks in the company's fleet. If everyone matched the new practice, a significant amount of fuel and emissions would be reduced.

It wasn't a manager who thought of this idea and put it into practice — it was a front-line employee. Who wouldn't want to open the door for people like Jim and his colleagues and give them a chance to show what they could do? There were tons of hidden gems among the 18,000 unionized employees at the company, and EPS could help them to emerge.

The Truth About Performance

A pragmatic business person would probably be muttering something right now about how performance reviews for unions are all very nice, but what's the pay off? Who needs another process which eats time? Why not just slip a little extra monetary reward to people at the end of the year and save all the effort? It's not a bad question. The problem is that the ROI on that money would be very uncertain.

It would be uncertain because of a hard truth about performance. When people do not get objective information and feedback about their job performance, they have no way of shaping it. When performance reviews are absent, research shows that mediocre employees think that they are the good performers, while the actual good performers tend to downplay their effectiveness.

Giving a bonus to people at the end of the year, rather than going through the tough work of performance reviews, might achieve exactly the opposite of what is desired. Mediocre performers would continue doing a middling job, and a bonus would deepen their false impression of their performance.

Nothing much would change with the good performers either. They're tougher on themselves, and if no one connected the extra money with information on how well they perform, they cannot redirect their efforts at company goals.

Nor would there be much progress with changing the culture in an organization in a positive direction. It's more likely that it would move back than go forward, because at the end of the day, while performance wouldn't have changed, business challenges get steeper all the time.

The Analysts' Meeting, November 2005

Here is the promise the analysts heard at the meeting from the SVP, HR:

"Most of our employees, about 90 per cent of them, do a good job. We actually have very few people who are a problem, and some of our employees go the extra mile without being asked.

Right now, our return on assets is the best in the industry. Imagine what could happen if we took that 90 per cent of employees doing a good job and helped them to do a great job. Imagine how our profitability would improve.

It has long been a dream for me to offer performance evaluations to unionized employees. Up until now, no one has told them how they are doing. We do performance evaluations for the non-union staff, but not the unionized people.

In 2006, that's going to change. I promise you that every one of our employees in the next year will receive a scorecard that measures them against our basic business principles. They'll be able to see how they are doing, and learn how they can do better.

The new performance evaluations will be called EPS. Now, to you, that means Earnings Per Share. But when you think about it, the individual performance of our employees is what adds up to make the company successful.

So EPS, Employee Performance Scorecards, produces EPS, Earnings Per Share. And by growing one, we'll grow the other."

CHAPTER 2

THE NIGHTMARE

It is a universal truth that once an idealistic dream comes into contact with reality, the nightmare begins. A living nightmare, one from which you can not wake up, no matter how hard you try. The nightmare may strike suddenly, with little to no warning. Paul tells how it happened to him:

"My boss came into my office after the November 2005 analysts' meeting in New York, and handed me a pair of custom napkin rings that were in the shape of the NYSE bulls. He said it was a gift from the meeting. I'm thinking to myself, 'Uh oh, a gift for no reason, this can't be good.' Then he just mentioned casually that he had made a promise at the analysts' meeting. He had told them that every unionized employee was going to get a performance appraisal in 2006.

And by the way, as I was running the Organizational Development part of the HR function, then I was in charge of making it happen. He knew it would be a big project, but he was sure that I and my team could handle it. Then he said he had a meeting and had to go, but before he left, he turned at the door, smiled and said 'good luck'.

I think time just stopped right then. I know my breathing did. I'm sure my eyes glazed over with shock. All I could think of was 'beware of a boss bearing a gift'."

It Can't Be Done, Part I

In the HR strategic plan, performance reviews for unionized employees was on the agenda. It was anticipated that the start date for the project would be sometime in late 2007, with the project taking about a year in development and then more time spent in running pilots. Actual delivery of the final product would probably take place two or three years later, depending on how many barriers were involved.

Given that future start date, there would be lots of opportunity to staff the project with enough people and fund it appropriately. There would be time to line up IT support and get the HR performance review project on their priority schedule. Lots of time to consult with all the operational folks and other affected parties, get their input and craft a system that would meet needs.

If an ill wind started to blow from some direction, then the project could be stalled until everyone was back on track and in agreement before proceeding. That way friction would be minimized, and with a lengthy head's up, everyone would be ready for the new initiative.

Beyond the accelerated timeline, there was another issue. In the particular nightmare that the HR team was having, there were no resources. No people available for the project, no budget and no space on the calendar to do it. The HR plan and priority list for 2006 was already full. True, a minor project could be wriggled in some how, but EPS was not a minor project.

To deliver the performance reviews by the end of 2006, the EPS project would have to run in double fast time. The pilot had to be done in the first quarter, and the training and reviews had to be delivered starting in the second quarter. No one in the field knew it was coming. No advance support for the project was in place.

All of these factors paled in comparison to one particular aspect of this nightmare. No one in HR had yet given any thought to the actual format of performance reviews for unionized employees. No one knew what it would look like, much less how to deliver 18,000 reviews within the year.

The HR team cried out in unison: "It can't be done!"

How Not to Make Friends

While HR doubted it could be delivered in a year, at least it was known to be on the future priority list. There was agreement that performance reviews for unionized people was a good idea in theory. In due time, it would fit in with larger culture change and, if handled correctly, a smooth transition from no reviews to formal reviews could be managed.

On the contrary, the operating people knew next to nothing about it. It wasn't a matter of not knowing what it would look like or how it would be delivered, they weren't even aware that it was coming.

December is not a good time to announce an unexpected initiative. Operational management already had their business plans in place for 2006. Their goals were ambitious, which gave them a steep challenge. It seemed unlikely that they would have the time or attention for a major change initiative.

Performance reviews would certainly be a surprise. Not the kind of nice surprise that comes in pretty wrapping paper, that you're pleased to see and happy to open. No, this kind of surprise might feel more like an ambush. The kind of surprise you don't want and are not the least bit pleased to encounter.

It Can't Be Done, Part II

With a trace of trepidation, Paul contacted the Divisional operational executives. They could see both the value of EPS and the problems of implementing it within one year. Their response was a muted "We're cautiously optimistic."

Somewhat encouraged, Paul began to contact a broader selection of key operating people to get the word out about EPS. He met with varying reactions. Some people "half-" smiled, and then chuckled.

"Keep on dreaming, Paul. It's always good to have a dream."

As Paul wasn't having a dream, he was having a nightmare, this response was a little irritating. He took it to mean that the operating people didn't have any sense of urgency about performance reviews, which was indeed correct, and didn't correspond to Paul's sense of urgency, which was off the Richter Scale.

There were a few "soothing" responses, exactly the kind you get when someone thinks that you're demented and they need to calm you. Then, there was the opposite reaction — screaming, yelling and shouting. Those reactions convinced Paul that the nightmare was real, especially when they were followed by a prompt apology. An apology meant that people believed what he was talking about was going to happen, and Paul still didn't know what it would look like or how to deliver it.

Operational managers are, on the whole, a pragmatic bunch. They work every day with potentially dangerous machinery, and balance time pressures and often contradictory demands to meet objectives. They keep their heads and coolly make decisions and solve problems. For many of the operating managers, some way would be found to manage EPS if it arrived on their doorstep.

Their pragmatism was welcomed, but the hurdles that the operating people were going to have leap were still there. Eighteen thousand performance reviews were going to eat time. Supervisors, already loaded to the max, would have to carve out the time to prepare and deliver the reviews. They would need to find extra time to be trained, and play a role in the communication chain. And they still had to do their jobs every day.

If EPS was going to work and deliver value, it needed to be done right. For a large organization, completing and delivering such a major project for the field in such a short time period was next to impossible. Even the best of intentions and the pragmatic problem-solving talents of operating management might not be sufficient.

Whether said aloud or silently, the operational groups thought pretty much the same as the HR group. "It can't be done."

CHAPTER 3

THE PERFORMANCE REVIEW TIME BLUES

The very nature of EPS added a little extra chill to the nightmare scenario facing the HR team. Performance reviews fall into an area of management practice which is typically haphazard. Of all the processes found within organizations, probably none come in for more abuse, misuse and neglect than a company's performance review system.

Just about every manager, at one or another time, sings the performance review time blues. When review time rolls around, the wailing of the blues can be heard from almost every corner of an organization. It's set to the tune of a funeral dirge, with a repetitive chorus.

"I haven't got the time."

"What should I say?"

"What will it change?"

There are legions of managers out there who will tell you that performance reviews are a waste of time. It's true that a badly done performance review is likely to yield a poor result. The alternative is true, too - a well done performance review makes a positive difference. The trick lies in understanding the difference between the two.

Truly Boneheaded Comments

Some of the following comments give a good picture of the entrenched beliefs that "leaders" hold about performance evaluation.

"If you tell people that they have performed well, then they won't work so hard. They'll coast."

"Giving performance reviews is asking for trouble. People want more money or a promotion if the review is good."

"It's better not to tell your staff exactly what you think of them. It puts a little tension into the work place if they don't know how you see them. Not knowing, keeps them on their toes. It makes them work harder, and try to please you more."

"The sure way to ruin good performers is to give them a good performance review."

These managers would tell you that they don't need to do reviews. They spend every day with their people, and they give them a ton of feedback. They ignore that most of their time is devoted to delegating, juggling resources, following-up on priorities and putting out fires.

Certainly managers spend a good deal of time communicating. It's just that much of that communication is tied to meeting short term objectives. There can be little daily communication about performance, and certainly not how it relates to people's learning needs, aspirations or dreams. All of that stuff, which is so important to employees, tends to get omitted.

And when employees don't get their performance acknowledged and recognized, they sing the blues, too. From the frontline to the executive suite, when good performance doesn't get acknowledged, the blues are wailed. The poor performers, of course, are just as happy to miss the reviews.

Performance reviews are not a substitute for day-to-day feedback and coaching from a manager. They are simply a stake in the ground, where employees can get a clear sense of objectives and expectations, and integrated feedback on their performance. Review time is the opportunity to talk about learning and development needs, and to talk about employees' future career aspirations.

So, why do so many people sing the blues about reviews?

Here Be Dragons

The problem with performance review systems is actually quite simple. It is not a process which tends to engage managers. This lack of engagement comes from managers seeing the process as:

- A mandated (read "empty") process rather than a business objective, which makes it of low importance;
- Consuming valuable time which could be spent better on more rewarding priorities;
- Having no immediate rewards — performance behavior does not change in an instant;
- Having the potential for conflict if employees don't like their reviews, which carries the risk that the sessions could be unpleasant; and,
- Having no real negative consequences for noncompliance, beyond a little grumbling from HR.

These factors do not support doing performance reviews. A process which has low importance, consumes time, and has no short term benefits is not a winner. Add in the potential for conflict and it becomes even less attractive. Instead, it is a process that is negative to managers, which increases their tendency to avoid it. The final point is that managers in most organizations are not held accountable when they fail to do the reviews, so that there are no adverse consequences which might make them think twice.

Skating on Thin Ice

Despite all the problems with performance reviews, the HR team believed in their importance. They knew that reviews could make a difference if done correctly. There was already a performance review system in place for management, and while it had been upgraded, there were still issues with it occasionally. Some managers failed to value it, and gave it short shrift. The team knew that some of the supervisors had this lack of care demonstrated in the performance evaluations that they received. It might be tough for them to catch the excitement of EPS if their past experience with reviews was poor.

As word began to filter out through back channels that EPS was coming, the faint humming of the performance review time blues began to be heard from the supervisors.

"I haven't got the time."

"What should I say?"

"What will it change?"

CHAPTER 4

AN UNCHARTED JOURNEY

The HR team wasn't stuck in the frame of Munch's The Scream for long. Once they got over the shock of the deadline on the EPS project, the nightmare faded. It was replaced quickly by anticipation, as the team began to relish the challenge of delivering the "Can't Be Done" .

The conviction grew that it could be done, even if the "how-to" part wasn't entirely certain yet. None of the company's competitors provided unionized employees with performance evaluations, so there wasn't an established path to follow. Indeed, very few large organizations do performance reviews with unionized staff. That absence of a map provided an opportunity to draw a new one and be creative.

Within HR, there was agreement that it was worth doing. There were far too many front-line employees who had worked in the company for decades and never got so much as a "thank you" for their efforts. Recognition for them on an individual level was past due.

From Abdication to Control

Once upon a time, managers lacked much interest in the business, because they didn't get rewarded by paying close attention to what was happening in the field. After the IPO, that behavior changed. They became very much on top of issues and in control of what people were doing. From not paying too much attention, they were working every lever possible to reach profit targets.

From the HR team's point of view, managers were too much in control of people. When management control dominates in an organization, employees are forced into compliance mode. Basically, it means that you follow orders or you will pay for it. With the focus on avoiding negatives outcomes, there isn't much will on the part of employees to go the extra mile.

The next step with culture change was to move to a work environment where people were informed and could become engaged. Employees who are committed to the business, and who have some feelings of ownership over their piece of it, pay more attention. EPS was a building block in the direction of that commitment.

The team was determined that EPS was not going to be a flavor of the month change initiative. Instead, it was going to be a key step on the path to culture change, with real power and high impact. Realistically, its full power wouldn't be apparent in the first year, but every journey has to start somewhere.

The Objectives of EPS

The objectives set for the design of EPS and the outcomes from it were ambitious.

- ***Align to Business Principles***

The company has five business principles which guide decisions made about the business. Front-line employees needed to be able to relate to these principles and feel that they were part of something larger than their day-to-day jobs. The principles had to go from being lofty corporate speak to having real meaning.

- ***Provide Recognition***

The company was fortunate to have a lot of talented employees in the unionized ranks, but HR was pretty sure that their contributions were not being recognized. It was time to say thank you to them, and treat them with the same respect and dignity that the other 20 percent (management staff) of the company received. The team dubbed it "giving the good people a hug".

- ***Be a Platform for Communication***

EPS would provide a clear cut opportunity for a conversation between supervisors and employees, where the emphasis was on the individual. Supervisors would find out a lot more about their employees, and the employees could discover that supervisors were human too. Ideally, this platform would help to open the door to ongoing discussions and collaboration on reaching goals, instead of orders followed by an empty "Yes, sir".

- ***Provide Clarity***

For people to be successful, they need a little help. They need clarity around their goals, and an understanding of how their performance will be evaluated. It doesn't do any good if these expectations are unspoken. EPS would allow goals to be specified, and expectations defined. Once clear measurements could be added into the process, people would be able to gauge their progress for themselves and shift their efforts as necessary.

- ***Identify Future Supervisory/Management Talent***

Like most companies, there was always a need for more and more supervisory and management talent. That need is only likely to grow in the future as baby boomers leave the work force. EPS would feature a segment on career interests and aspirations, which could help identify people who were interested in leadership roles.

- ***Be an Upgrade for the Supervisors***

A side benefit of EPS would be to deepen the skills of supervisors. Just about all of them had received basic training in their roles, and doing performance evaluations was another opportunity to apply it. It would all be part of the culture agenda to increase the rate of feedback to employees, and learn to be more comfortable in doing it. The goal was for them to stop giving orders, and start to influence behavior and shape it.

- ***Improve Business Results***

EPS offered another way for managers to enhance business results. The company had gone a long way down the road of profitability, but if another 18,000 people worked on it, the team was sure that results would be even better. EPS could be the start of shifting people from taking orders to thinking like intrepreneurs. The goal was to insure that every employee in the company was part of the feedback loop from vision to action to results.

CHAPTER 5

WHAT WENT BEFORE

The company operates across Canada and the U.S. It's a vast amount of geographic ground to cover. With such far flung operations, it can be difficult for everyone to stay on the same path and work in a co-ordinated fashion. Joe, who works in Alberta, will probably never meet or even talk to Mary who works in Michigan, or Tyler in Kansas. Yet they all have to share a common understanding of what is required to make the business work.

To get people to think in a similar way, to use the same criteria in making decisions or solving problems, without losing sight of local issues, is any company's toughest journey. It always involves huge cultural change, and the disruption that goes with it.

There is a saying that if you want to eat an elephant, you do it one piece at a time. The same holds true for culture change. It's done best when one piece is brought in at a time, digested, and then another is linked to it. Before EPS was introduced, there had already been a steady diet of culture change.

1. — The Base
Five Business Principles

A new CEO brought a set of business principles with him. They were formulated to provide some "rules of the road" for people to help them make decisions about running the company, whether those decisions were made in Toronto or Vancouver. They are, as principles, far from prescriptive, but they provide people with a common language and help them frame how to think about issues. These principles were the first step in culture change.

Customer Service

In the beginning and in the end, the business is about serving customers. It's about engaging customers through communication, understanding their needs and making commitments that are kept. When mistakes happen, it's all about taking responsibility and being accountable for making it right. By serving customers, the shareholders are served also.

Process Flexibility

Every business needs the right processes in place to run in the most efficient way. All of the business and operating processes in a company need to be rethought continuously to improve them and be fine-tuned to stay in harmony with external and internal change. It's not about cutting out the last dollar; it's about leveraging each dollar available.

Be Wise with Assets

Assets are all the things that are thought of typically, like machinery, raw materials and buildings, and some things that don't get thought of automatically, like people, filing cabinets and office cubicles. Effective asset utilization means having exactly what is needed to run the business, with no asset underutilized, which turns that asset into a liability. It doesn't mean doing without; it means making the best use of the assets available.

Keep Everybody Safe

Safety comes first, for the sake of employees, the communities in which they live, customers and the environment. It means having clear cut processes to follow, and being in compliance with safety and operating rules all of the time. Safety is good for the business.

People Count

Without the people who work at the company, there would no business. It's important to attract the right people, develop them, communicate expectations and results to them and engage them. It's all about growing leadership capabilities, from the top of the organization to the front-line.

This base step meant for the first time that everyone could share the same understanding of how to think about and operate the business. It was a road map to follow.

2. — The Next Step
The ABC's of Management Behavior

The next hurdle in culture change was to get consistency in the behavior of managers. It seemed that there were dozens of different management styles in place throughout the company. Some people had been exposed to formal training. Others had taught themselves how to manage, unfortunately sometimes using a bad boss as an example of how to behave.

In some eyes, the company's management style seems to be based upon the military model. It involves being in control and giving orders. The expected response from employees is "Yes sir, no sir." The comparison to this model breaks down when it comes to the heavy emphasis the military places upon the welfare of their troops. Officers don't get far in the military if they don't make sure their troops are ready for whatever comes their way, have the resources for the job and feedback on their performance.

The Need in a Nutshell

"I have good operating people. They know how to run the system. What I don't always have are good leaders. I need every leader to know how to coach and motivate their people."

A senior Operations executive

The varying management styles in place were definitely a problem. It confused people, and often resulted in management behavior which was in direct contradiction to stated goals. The competency of managers needed to grow for the company to grow the business.

The vehicle chosen to get all managers acting alike was behavioral based management training, offered by CLG Consultants. While the thinking behind their training was grounded in academic theory, the application of it was purely practical. It started with the executive group, then the training was cascaded down through the management ranks to supervisors.

Managers in the company use **A**ntecedents, such as training, verbal instructions or information, to trigger **B**ehaviors by people that will lead to goal attainment. Managers then apply Consequences, either positive or negative, to sustain or reshape behavior. The emphasis is on reinforcing behavior through positive outcomes, as behavior which is rewarded is most likely to be repeated and become ingrained.

Management by Accident

All managers, whether they know it or not, use behavioral methods. Take the case of Joe Doe, whose direct report, Jake, did not meet his performance goals in his first year of employment. Joe didn't want to "demotivate" Jake, so at the end of the year he gave him a raise. Then he wondered why Jake's performance didn't improve. Of course, what Joe had done was reward poor performance, making it much more likely it would be repeated.

With the disciplined use of the ABC model, the company made good progress in changing behavior and improving performance. Managers learned that antecedents carry only 20% of the weight in achieving objectives, although traditionally that is where they put most of their attention. Now, they're more focused on consequences, which account for 80% of outcomes. It has forced managers to pay attention to what people are doing, to coach for desired results and communicate through frequent feedback. EPS would help keep this momentum going, especially for the first-line supervisors.

3. — Refining the Model
Q4 Thinking

The fundamental purpose of a leader is to achieve results. There's no question about the purpose of the role. It's how those results are achieved that matters. To help managers understand more about how to achieve results that maximized people's efforts, the concept of Q1 to Q4 thinking, also from CLG, was introduced.

Q3 Gets short-term business results People are disengaged	Q4 Good business results People are engaged
Q1 Poor with business results Poor with people	Q2 Poor with business results Effective with people

The model describes four different modes of management functioning. Basically, a leader at the Q1 level doesn't get good results, nor has an effective people management style. So the business is failing slowly, and employees are disengaged. Leaders at the Q2 stage don't get good business results either, but they do treat people well. Employees are comfortable with this leader, although they may soon be looking for work as the business crumbles.

A Q3 leader gets business results that may look good on the surface, but any gains are usually short term and can't sustain a company over time. People following the orders of a Q3 leader keep their heads down and avoid involvement, because the style of the Q3 leader is punitive. These leaders get results, which can blind companies to the real long-term damage that they do.

A Q4 leader is balanced, with positive outcomes with both the business and people. This leader recognizes that results have to be achieved through people and can adapt to employees who are at different stages in their development. A Q4 leader can coach an employee to develop new skills and learn, or variously motivate an experienced person who needs more challenge. When necessary, Q4 leaders don't hesitate to take action on poor performance. So this stage of leadership doesn't mean being soft on people, but requires leaders to vary the styles and methods they use to lead people to good business results.

This concept was one more way of getting out the message that good business results come from managing people effectively. In the long run, an organization can't continue to grow unless that balance is present. By identifying where managers were on the Q1 to Q4 spectrum, they knew what they needed to work on, and very specific coaching plans could be put in place.

Another Step

The poets say that to everything there is a time and a season, and the same was true of EPS. If HR had tried to introduce the concept several years earlier, it would have been laughed out of the room. At that time, the majority of managers were still at the Q3 stage of command and control. Q3 leaders don't think that they have to offer recognition to their people, or thank them for doing a good job. They believe that people ought to offer thanks for having a job.

By 2006, the transition from having mostly Q3 leaders, who were best at command and control, to Q4 leaders, was well underway. Q4 leaders have a better appreciation of what people can do in an organization, and value them. They tend to give feedback on an ongoing basis, and EPS was a chance to recognize good performance on a formal basis.

In effect, EPS was positioned to build on the earlier culture change that managers had experienced. It would give supervisors a chance to make the Five Business Principles meaningful to the field. Supervisors could utilize the feedback skills they'd learned through ABC training. It all added up to a good foundation for EPS. Despite the performance review time blues being hummed in the background, it was the right time and the right season.

CHAPTER 6

PUTTING IT IN THE FRAME

Once the senior people in the divisions had made a commitment to EPS, the HR team was satisfied that the groundwork was in place to proceed with the project. There was more work to do in getting the messages down and filtered through the organization, but the commitment of the senior people was the first key to success.

EPS was a huge project to do in less than one year. It was not going to be possible to follow traditional project management methods. Those methods, which rely on sequential steps to get from the beginning to the end, were too time-consuming. Instead, multiple steps would have to be completed in parallel. That choice ramped up the complexity of an already complicated undertaking, but it was the only way to finish this project on time.

To make EPS happen, the team had to figure out what the project's role was in larger culture change. Then, what it would look like. From there, decisions could be made about how to deliver it. Along the way, there were going to be hundreds of decisions, problems and details to manage, all of which the team would have to handle as they happened.

The Project Guidance Committee

Paul formed a Guidance Committee. He wanted, right at the start of the project, to have a wide view of possibilities for EPS.

In the end, technical expertise would be necessary to create the product, deliver and support it. The technical side of EPS, however, was just one aspect. EPS was part of culture change, and had to fit into the strategic thinking around it. EPS also had to add value to the business, and it was important that divisional field issues were not missed.

CLG (Continuous Learning Group) Consultants were brought in as an initial partner in the project. They were already working in the company to help upgrade the effectiveness of managers through the ABC and Q4 training. As they worked with a wide range of clients, CLG had seen many different performance review systems. They would have an informed idea of what methods would work best in performance evaluation, and what should be avoided. They could provide an overview to the Guidance Committee as a whole as it developed the EPS strategy.

Company HR people were the other initial part of the Guidance Committee. They had the networks and connections within the organization to gather information and shape EPS in relation to the company's needs. They knew the intricacies of the company's structure and politics, and how to work around hurdles. Field management was already an HR client, and there was enough trust built to support the implementation of EPS.

The thinking behind the composition of the committee was to combine CLG's broad consulting overview with HR's technical expertise and practical knowledge of the company. By balancing the different perspectives, the team could maximize the strategic contribution of EPS to culture change. It could also build a robust product that helped the business.

The "Yes, But" Hurdle

The first hurdle with any committee is getting everyone aligned. At the initial meeting of the Guidance Committee most people did seem to be aligned, at least based on their comments.

"It's a great idea. But it can't be done in the time frame."

"It fits with all the culture change we're doing, but it can't be done in a year."

"I can see the value, but I can't see how we're going to do it."

Paul decided that this alignment was not desirable. "If we put all our energy into "yes, but" thinking, we'll never get it done. The senior people have made a commitment to it. Don't look at why we can't do it. Ignore why we can't do it. If none of those things existed, what would we do? Look at it that way."

There was no more time wasted on "yes, but" comments. The Committee went to work.

Framing the Project

The first step was to build a clear framework for the EPS project. On the one hand, broad thinking and discussion was necessary, so there would definitely be some blue sky imagining. Realistically, there was a need to be pragmatic, given the timeline and finite resources.

The solution was to build a vision for EPS that would be achieved over five years. That solution allowed the thinking around EPS to be far ranging, and build into the new process the best practices in performance evaluation. The team quickly became comfortable with the idea that the first year would be "launch mode", with antenna on full alert for practical issues.

Successive years would allow EPS to be deepened and evolve to match larger cultural change.

This framework helped on two fronts. By having a clear understanding of what EPS would be down the road, choices could be made in the launch year that lined up with the end vision. By knowing that there were opportunities to build and shape EPS over time, the immediate focus could stay on practical launch needs.

Seven Rules

Every project needs guidelines, especially one with the complexity of EPS and the need to deliver it in a short time period. The team developed these seven rules to help guide the project.

Employees Get Thanked

The company had learned to deal with poor performers and bad actors since the IPO, albeit in a pretty harsh way. While that segment of the employee population was small, it created a lot of noise. In turn, that noise attracted management attention.

The goal was for EPS to shift the attention away from people who acted out, to people who did a good job. They are the ones that really count.

The project team believed that 90 percent or better of unionized employees did a good job. They believed also that frontline workers didn't get the recognition that they deserved for their efforts, or a clear "Thank you".

Everyone Gets a Scorecard

Employees would benefit from having a tangible reminder of their EPS session. Being a new experience for employees and supervisors, everyone was likely to be a little nervous. As a result, employees might not be able to remember every word that was said during their session.

At the end of the session, employees would be handed a scorecard. It needed to look good and feel substantial in their hand. It was an important record for them, and written recognition of their efforts.

Create No New Measures

Effective performance evaluations are based on objective data. The objective was to use existing data in the company's systems.

There were two obvious benefits to this data rule. For the project team, it meant that a good pace could be maintained, as the data could be accessed readily. For the supervisors, it meant that they would be using familiar measures. If new measures were introduced into operations over time, EPS could adopt them, but would not create them.

Do no harm

Some people in the field had come back with an initial reaction of "We don't need it," or "No one else does it, why should we?" The team was in vehement disagreement with such sentiments, and saw them as resistance to change in disguise. The company did need it, and while the timing might have been a surprise, EPS was the right thing to do.

Comments that were of greater concern ran along the lines of "We don't know how to do it," or "We're so busy, how can we do it right?" The intention behind EPS was not to make it hard for supervisors, but to give them a tool to help them manage performance and results. The goal was to help them do it right.

There is a tendency for people to see the act of giving feedback as potential for conflict. So supervisors were disinclined to give unvarnished opinions to their direct reports, yet might hold negative perceptions of them. That behavior harmed employees and the business. An effective EPS system would help both sides of the equation.

Support the Supervisors

It seemed likely that not all of the supervisors would be entirely familiar with performance evaluations. Reviews had only reached the first-line supervisory level a few years before the EPS project, and they weren't done consistently. Without in-depth personal experience with the process, they might not have a high personal comfort level with it.

The supervisors couldn't be thrown cold into EPS. They would require training, documentation and support.

Survive the Year

This rule was made for the team. Any big project like EPS is exhausting, but it's not just a matter of physical survival.

Everyone on the team was an old hand with big projects. They knew that things go wrong, and they usually go wrong at the most inconvenient moment. There was a certain amount of skepticism in the organization about EPS in general, and in particular about implementing it in a year. By proposing EPS, HR was making a commitment to employees. It needed to do what it said it would do.

There was also the need to handle some of the team members' tendency toward perfectionism. As this was just the launch year, any mistakes could be solved in the next round of performance reviews.

Create a Base for the Future

Putting in a solid foundation for EPS in the launch year was important. It needed to be accepted into the culture, and become part of the language. If the team built a good foundation, the process would have value and benefits, and there would be receptivity to its further growth.

The intention was that every year EPS could get deeper. Supervisors would develop their capacity to set clear goals and articulate expectations. The relevance and meaningfulness of the feedback would get stronger. Employees would get recognition, and they would also have a chance for coaching and development to help them be as successful as they wanted.

The Vision

EPS was one more progressive step to fit into the cultural change at the company. It had to be aligned with the company's Business Principles, the ABC training and the Q4 approach to leadership.

When it was finished completely, EPS would have distinct features:

- Performance data would be collected in one, easily accessible system;
- Scorecards would be customized by each individual's job;

- Feedback would be a meaningful blend of objective and qualitative data;
- Positive consequences would reward employees and supervisors;
- Constructive feedback would shape performance and development;
- Two-way conversations would define clear expectations for next steps;
- Employees' possible career objectives would be included;
- EPS could be renewed and refreshed to keep pace with other change;
- Ultimately EPS would include an assessment by employees of their leaders' ability to provide effective feedback; and,
- Performance evaluation would become expected and the norm at all levels within the organization.

The Guidance Committee achieved all of these outputs in the first meeting. During the active launch year, the vision of what EPS could be remained steady.

After the vision was set, the nature of the Guidance Committee changed. While it started with external consultants and internal HR people, operational people were invited to come in as well. Their input and ideas were vital.

With all of these voices, the Guidance Committee became huge. With the vision clear and set, energy had to be redirected into getting the project done. While the committee deliberations went on in successive meetings, it was time to translate words into action.

CHAPTER 7

THE STEALTH PROJECT TEAM

By the time that EPS was conceived, the company had already dealt with an immense amount of change. Introducing change into the organization was not a new endeavor, but with EPS the pattern shifted. It was not only going to be change. EPS was going to be change done in a different way.

Paul tells how the introduction of change had been managed previously in the company:

"In the past, whenever we brought in change, we did it selectively. The company is huge on a national basis, but it's got lots of nooks and crannies. There are three big divisions, and they're all different. Nor is everything centralized by geography, so not every function works out of head office.

What you had to do when you wanted to bring in change was to find the group or division who wanted it. Somewhere in the company there was always a place that was ready for change, and looking for it. You might have to whisper in someone's ear to make sure they knew that they were ready for change, but once they heard you, then they were open to it.

Previously, that openness to change was how we picked the places to pilot change. It was more of a pull from a specific location than a push from corporate. Once it got started and worked, the new behaviors would get recognized and rewarded. Then people from other locations would come and demand the change. Then it would spread throughout the entire organization."

With EPS, the change was coming via a push from corporate. No one was out there asking for it or demanding it. This change introduction was going to be different, and maybe a little bit trickier. For one thing, operations had to be prepared for it before the product was ready or even defined totally.

HR Goes It Alone

EPS was the first time that major change had been brought into the company without the benefit of a task force. There was no time for a task force, which typically on a project of this size can take a year or so to come up with an introduction-ready product. The idea of following a standard task force protocol with the implementation was abandoned immediately. HR was going to freestyle.

There was not going to be an opportunity to maximize the use of consultants, which many large organizations draft when they need extra hands. Resources were scarce, and HR was going to have to handle the implementation phase without much help. They already had existing relationships with operating people, which could be drawn on to buy some latitude as EPS unfolded. If there were problems, they could be negotiated on the spot. If it was necessary to tweak or modify the project, the team could use its judgment and knowledge of the company to do it.

HR stepped into the driver's seat. A lean and mean stealth team, it could move faster than any committee task force. There might have to be the occasional apology for the turbulence that the team caused on occasion, but the determination to get it done was high.

How The Team Lived to Tell the Tale

Paul, Cathy and Sara comprised the nucleus of the EPS team. If you were to ask them how they got the project done in a year, they would reply with a shrug and say, "We just did it."

That statement makes it sound like everything went smoothly, like a stroll in the park. In reality, there were occasions when to describe the project as sometimes messy, frustrating, and confusing would be polite understatement.

In debriefing the team at the end of the project, some themes emerged which they think helped to account for the success:

- ***A Guiding Belief***

Everyone believed in the benefits that EPS could bring to individual employees and to the organization. EPS was the next needed step in the company's culture change story, which made it critically important. That belief never faded, and was a source of energy in influencing people who did not yet believe in EPS.

- ***A Shared Vision***

The initial work of the Project Committee had crafted a strong vision for EPS. Parts of the how-to's were changed and tweaked as the team progressed, but the vision itself never altered. When in a tight spot and trying to sort through alternatives to make the best choices for EPS, the Seven Rules provided answers.

- ***It's All About Perception***

There are always bumps in the road and unexpected detours on a large project. If you see them as barriers, the project grinds to a halt. If you see them as hurdles, you have options. You can go over, around or under a hurdle. It's all in how you see things. The team chose to see hurdles, not barriers.

- ***Decisions in the Hallways***

Formal meetings take time, which was in short supply. Instead, as team members met in the hallways, they talked as they went, and made decisions on the spot. Heads were popped around office doors, with focused discussions leading to fast decisions. The definition of a meeting was shifted from a scheduled time in a particular place with a pre-set agenda to any way the team could connect on priorities.

- ***The Virtue of Impatience***

According to the CEO, "Patience is overrated as a virtue. People are too damn patient around here, when they should be taking action." No one has ever successfully accused the high achievers on the HR team of being patient. Once there is agreement on a goal, they want to do it, and do it now. Fortunately, this impatience is tempered by perfectionism, so there is real effort put into doing it right.

- ***Asking for Forgiveness***

The team took full advantage of that old adage of "asking for forgiveness, rather than asking for permission." Paul and his group were moving so fast that they blew past normal processes and procedures in the organization. There were times when initiative was exercised and things got done that were not authorized fully or according to the rule book. There was always a prompt apology to anyone disgruntled by this behavior.

- ***Persistently Flexible***

If you can't always see what's coming, and surprises come tumbling out, you have to be persistent. While no one even thought of giving up, the team found it was necessary to be flexible. That flexibility was both with handling surprises, and giving room to colleagues. The team had strong opinions, and have been known to argue about them. They had to give up that habit and develop a new one, where everyone built on each others' ideas.

Running Fast in Parallel

At the start, there was some role confusion. Decisions were being made so fast that it was next to impossible to get the word out about what was happening and who was to do what task. After a little snarling about people butting in where they weren't wanted or needed, more role clarity was achieved. There was no time for duplication of efforts.

The team needed every hand available, and each hand had to manage the task of working in parallel to one another. While everyone in the team was welcome to offer input, a set of roles was developed that would cover the project efficiently and keep everyone focused.

Roles evolved as the needs and the ability to meet those needs became apparent. The stealth team was configured to be a small core of experts, and they drafted in more support as it became necessary. At different times, almost every HR person, in head office or out in the divisions, participated in the project in one capacity or another. That approach allowed the small group to reach out and get the specific help or the knowledge they needed at key points in the project. It also helped to keep some semblance of control with the project, because the team knew who was doing what.

The pilots were set to run in March. From the middle of January to March, the main components of EPS had to be tackled systematically. Within that time frame the segments were:

- Plan and start a communication program;
- Work networks to build engagement for EPS;
- Inform the unions;
- Develop the performance measures;
- Find the performance data;
- Develop a program to run the data;
- Create the scorecard;
- Design the training;
- Train the pilots' trainers;
- Produce the pilots' training materials; and
- Think through the logistics of the rollout.

It was a long list to tackle, especially when everything had to be done simultaneously. As people got involved in the project, they had to be free to evolve their thinking as they went. There wasn't time to take every decision back to a committee and hash it out in a meeting. Without that ability to double-check and confirm, there was a risk that information gaps might appear. A small team made it easier to manage.

The Blessing of a Small Team

"It didn't take too long," Paul says,

"Before we were able to," Sara adds,

"Finish each other's sentences." Cathy concludes.

CHAPTER 8

GO TELL IT

Change has been a constant companion for the company in the last decade, and EPS was another major one that was coming people's way. It was an exciting and significant one, but still a change.

When change is the norm, people live with ambiguity. Some people thrive on it; others see it as a cold wind. Shelter from the wind will come once people understand new demands and learn how to respond to them. Getting everyone to that point at roughly the same time is at the core of change management. To manage that feat, you have to tell the right story about it.

Communication about change is vital, not optional. As people that have gone through transformative changes will tell you, when change is on the table, you need to communicate, communicate and communicate again. It is impossible to communicate too much.

Thinking about Communication

There is an invisible barrier with communication about change. Quite often, people just don't want to hear about it. While the status quo may not be perfect, there is a comfort level with it. People know what to expect and what to do. It's not necessary to do any new learning, or the even harder task of unlearning.

Change messages can also be difficult to hear because of all the competing noise in the workplace. Immediate priorities carry more weight with people because they are real, and need to be dealt with now. Change is in the future and has a hazy outline. Sure, it's out there, but will it ever arrive?

Communication about change is like a rehearsal for the change itself. It sets the tone, and when done skillfully it can answer questions before they become burning issues. It serves as a frequent reminder that change is coming, and helps to fill in some of that hazy outline.

One of the first things done in the EPS project was to think about how to communicate about this new change. Given the inflexible end date, it was necessary to work backwards from it to map out a schedule for developing the mechanics of the process, piloting it and implementing it. The team drafted in a colleague who was an expert in communication. He took responsibility for initiating communications, while the rest of the team worked on other elements of the project.

The Stakeholders

To make communication work, you have to know your audience. Communication is all about influencing others. It's not about talking down to people or talking over them, but rather talking directly to them. Core messages must be consistent with everyone, with fine-tuning to fit the "What's in it for me?" for each audience.

The two primary audiences were:

- **Unionized employees**

Typically, the company's unionized employees had decades of experience on the job, but little to no experience with formal feedback. When they had received feedback, it was most likely focused on mistakes and negative in nature. This audience was likely to wonder how easy it would be to listen to performance feedback, and be skeptical of the value of the process.

- **First-line supervisors**

This group would have the new responsibility of giving formal performance feedback to the employees. They might be wondering about how well they could deliver it. EPS would be also a new priority added to their already busy workloads. Within this context, it would be important to build their belief in the value of the process and support them.

The secondary audiences were:

- **Union Leaders**

They had genuine concerns about EPS and what it might mean, especially if it turned out to be discipline in disguise. Their primary concern was likely to be if unintended consequences from this change left them looking like they had failed to protect the unionized employees.

- **Investors/Analysts**

Building strong, effective leadership has been at the heart of the company's culture change journey. The analysts would be interested in any tactic which increased leadership capability and helped to differentiate the company further from the competition.

- **Company Management**

Without management backing, EPS would be reduced to the ignominious graveyard of change — just another flavor of the month idea. Negative noise that filters up through the ranks can make managers uneasy, and they would need information to answer questions.

Creating Awareness

With the large numbers of stakeholders who needed to know about EPS, the communication plan had to be comprehensive, with as many chances as possible to reach people. The first step in the communication plan was to get the message out about the arrival of EPS.

The objective in creating awareness was for EPS to become associated with the company's overall People strategy. It was important that the project didn't seem like a one time special event, which would be talked about and then would disappear. Rather than create a special program which featured EPS alone, information about it was integrated into the regular communication vehicles available within the company about people and the company's culture journey. In this way, EPS drove the communication and became entwined with the bigger story.

The Initial Message

"This year will mark a new People initiative for the company. For the first time, we will be introducing an employee performance evaluation for unionized employees. Unionized employees will be able to receive feedback on their individual performance from their supervisor. The process will be called Employee Performance Scorecard (EPS), and create an opportunity for employees to have positive feedback and recognition for their efforts.

The vast majority of our unionized employees do good work, each and every day, and positive recognition for them is well deserved. EPS will help also to identify unionized employees who are interested in supervisory roles in the future. As the company continues to grow and expand in its markets, we need more leaders. EPS will be a mechanism to help us identify people who want to shape their careers to include leadership roles."

An excerpt from the company's first quarter's employee magazine, 2006

Most audiences need to hear a new message three times before it really catches their attention. In tandem with the EPS project schedule, messages were presented in the normal communication channels:

- The company's quarterly magazine to all employees;
- Bi-weekly electronic bulletins to keep everyone updated;
- Divisional newsletters;
- Quarterly results reports; and

- The monthly People Priorities Report from HR.

A Message for the U.S. Division

"With our new Employee Performance Scorecard program, unionized employees and their supervisors will meet to review the past year and receive personalized feedback on their performance. It will also be a chance to think about the coming year and identify performance goals for it. Every employee will be given a scorecard that details their performance feedback in writing. The Division plans to identify candidates through this interactive discussion who are interested in future supervisory roles."

An excerpt from the U.S. Division's newsletter, Spring 2006

In addition, a presentation was prepared for supervisors that they could share with their employees. It included financial results, so everyone was kept updated on the company's progress toward yearly business targets. The second section of the presentation was on the company's five business principles, with EPS being featured as a People Count initiative. It was a subtle way of educating the supervisors and the unionized ranks at the same time.

Making it Positive

In most work settings, people are flooded with messages, all of which compete for attention. An indirect source of competition is what is going on in people's heads, based on their past experience and knowledge. As a result, there can be a hidden positive or negative mindset before communication even starts.

With EPS, the objective was to foster positive feelings about the process.

Definitely, there needed to be a counter to the grapevine. Usually, a grapevine is full of rumours and speculation, and is often dismissed by management. It is easy to overlook that a grapevine is also a reflection of people's opinions and their interpretations of what they see and hear. While this information may not be factually correct, it plays a role in influencing people.

Even before the HR project team was certain about what EPS would actually look like, opinions about it were floating through the grapevine. In particular, EPS was being portrayed as a hidden discipline program. It seemed likely that this specific threat was being promoted by some union leaders, but to some extent negative rumors were part of the company's culture.

Like most organizations, the company has a certain percentage of cynical and disgruntled employees. They tend to be quite vocal in expressing their dissatisfaction. In the past, management had focused on responding to these unhappy people, not the employees who were satisfied with their jobs. As part of the communication strategy, it was important to emphasize the positive to set a new tone.

The HR team estimated that 90 per cent of unionized workers would be rated as skilled or outstanding employees. So, it wasn't just daydreaming that the majority of employees were capable and hardworking, and that EPS would be a positive experience for them.

The CEO Provides Support to EPS

"We have a history in this company of taking hard work by our unionized employees for granted. We don't always pay enough attention to their individual contributions, or let them know how much their efforts are appreciated and vital to the company. There's a formal performance evaluation done with managers, that let's them know how they've done, but not one for unionized employees.

Starting this year, unionized employees are going to have the same advantage of knowing how their performance is seen, and getting feedback on their achievements. We're calling it "Employee Performance Scorecard", because it's the efforts of every individual employee in the company that add up to us achieving our business goals at the end of the year.

We're setting a very ambitious agenda with EPS. None of our competitors do it. In fact, few companies include the unionized ranks when it comes to giving personal feedback and talking about development or career growth. But when it comes right down to it, all our employees count and all our people are going to be included in company-wide performance evaluations."

An excerpt from Spring 2006 the company's *People Are Talking* magazine

It was a good story to tell. Employees were getting the news long before the final format of EPS was ready for them. While the impending change created some trepidation, it also created a high level of interest. People were curious about what EPS would be like, and curiosity leads to engagement.

CHAPTER 9

UNION BUY-IN ... OR NOT

As the regional HR teams contacted operational managers to follow-up on the initial communications about EPS, they discovered something strange. Many of the managers in the field were worry-free about EPS, and had few questions about it. The HR folks found this relaxed response a bit unusual, as a high level of angst was the normal result of a major change initiative.

With some probing, HR discovered why so many operational managers were in a relaxed state of mind about EPS. They had no concerns about the short timelines on the project or the work load it might generate for them. Instead, they thought it simply couldn't happen. The unions would not permit it. They'd stop it long before the managers had to deal with it.

It was probably the first time many of the managers thanked their lucky stars for the presence of strong unions within the organization. Normally, most of them saw the unions as hazards to be navigated with care. Some managers thought that the unions interfered with getting a good day's effort out of employees. They believed the unions had too much power in protecting employees when they made mistakes or needed disciplinary action.

It was a telling response from managers. It suggested that they saw the unions as their adversaries. And, somewhere along the line, they seemed to have ceded ownership of the unionized employees to the unions.

EPS was a good opportunity to correct that thinking.

Taking a Stand

It was true that EPS was all about unionized employees. It was true also that anything that touched those employees was going to be of great concern to the unions. Union interest was expected as the unions were representing the interests of their members.

Senior management was not, however, prepared to cede the right to have a conversation with employees. While the employees might be members of a union, it was the company that paid them. It was the company that provided such things as tuition assistance, health benefits and pensions. It was clear that these employees worked for the company, and not for the unions.

In considering how to approach the unions about EPS, it was necessary to think through how they would respond. After all, the unions were partners in the business. It is as much in any union's best interests as in the company's to make sure that the business is healthy and profitable. A strong, growing company keeps workers employed. A company that goes down leaves unions with no one on the payroll to represent.

Accordingly, there is common ground shared with the unions, and agreement is not always elusive. All the same, there are times when some fundamentally different philosophies can open a divide between a company and its unions. Due to mergers and acquisitions over the years, multiple unions represented employees, which increased how many different perspectives would come into play with the introduction of EPS.

Differing Perspectives

Unions are collective endeavors, based upon the principle of equality. The union's philosophy is that everyone is equal, delivers the same performance and is entitled to equal treatment and rewards. The solidarity that is achieved through equality allows a union to speak as one voice for employees. It is that one voice that negotiates contracts with the company, and then each individual employee has the opportunity to vote on the result. It is a form of democracy in action.

It's hard to argue against the principle of equality. In truth, though, not everyone is equally competent or works equally hard. With EPS, the company was exercising its right to speak directly to all employees about performance. If there was a threat from EPS, it would likely come from the inconvenient reality that while everyone has equal rights, not everyone performs equally.

Taking It to the Unions

Just to make working with the unions more complex, labour law and regulations are different in Canada and the U.S. What you may be able to do in one country, you can't in the other, and vice versa. When it came to letting the unions know about EPS, they were approached in each country separately. The tactics used were different, and the reactions were different.

In the U.S.A.

There's a difference between informing and consulting. In the U.S., the choice was to consult. All of the union leaders were approached separately to discuss the idea of EPS. Their opinions were invited, and there was enough discussion to yield an understanding of what shaped those opinions. On the whole, there was a positive reaction from the union leaders.

Union leaders in the U.S. had been pointing out for some time that the company didn't pay attention to the ideas of unionized employees. They thought, correctly, that the employees had some important things to say, and there wasn't enough two way communication going on between supervisors and their people. If EPS allowed for open conversations, then it wouldn't be a bad thing, and management would know more about what was happening on the ground.

Through the consultation process, some suggestions were offered that might improve EPS. There was very little push back, but there were concerns on the part of some leaders that EPS was just another form of discipline. When that issue was a concern, there were repeated conversations until they understood fully that EPS was designed to be constructive.

At the end of the consultation process, the fears about discipline were laid to rest. There was enough union buy-in to proceed.

The Duty of Representation

It doesn't matter what side of the U.S./Canadian border it is when it comes to the unions' responsibility to represent the best interests of employees. In both countries, it is the law for unions to undertake the duty of representation on behalf of employees. Failure to do so can result in serious sanctions against a union. HR was well aware of this duty, which was why right from the beginning it was intended that EPS was not going to be about discipline.

North of the Border

In Canada, EPS was made a sidebar conversation at a regularly scheduled review meeting with union leaders. In that conversation, the union leaders were informed that performance evaluations with unionized employees would occur in 2006. Basically, they were told that EPS was going to happen whether or not they liked it.

Their reaction was not a happy one. They resisted the idea forcefully and immediately. Their first perception was that EPS was a way to weed out bad employees, and a back door to discipline. It wouldn't be a management tool to benefit employees, but rather a management tool that would undermine them.

Another part of what made them unhappy was the idea of a conversation between a supervisor and a unionized employee without a union representative being present. They wanted to know what was being said to any employee, and to listen to the conversation. That presence would help them to be able to continue their role in interpreting the company position to the union ranks.

There was some work to do to calm the waters. Quite frankly, with the short timeline for EPS, informing instead of consulting felt like it would be easier. Just like it's a lot easier to say "No" than to say "Yes", which is how the Canadian unions responded to the idea of EPS. Now, there really was a problem to fix.

A Sea of Grievances

Some of the Canadian unions didn't waste any time in filing grievances. There was no basis in labour law for the grievances;

rather the unions based them on the collective agreements. The central issue which propelled the grievances was discipline.

The union leaders' primary fear was that employees might say something in a performance discussion which would later be used against them. A careless comment, an admission of not doing something correctly, and it would be a "gotcha" moment.

Management could then sneak around due process, using the conversation or the documentation from the performance appraisal session. A union representative has the right to be present during a discipline discussion, as a support to the union member. If it turned out that there was a disciplinary element in EPS, the unions were concerned about being excluded from the sessions with the employee and the supervisor.

A second concern was what would happen if an employee was unhappy with their performance rating. Would that dissatisfaction be aimed at the union for not representing them in the session? A union is, after all, an institution, and every institution has politics. The union wanted to be present in the session to avoid that possibility by being able to participate in the discussion and challenge assessments.

A third concern was that EPS was change, which challenges the status quo in ways that are unpredictable. In Canada, the process was presented as a unilateral change, which didn't sit well. After all, the leaders are elected to their offices by the unionized employees. Excluded from participation in the shaping of EPS, the union leaders' only chance to influence this change was to grieve it. At the end of the day, they needed to look active in the eyes of their constituents, or they could be voted out at the next election.

Repair Work

Individual union leaders were approached quietly, and discussions took place. Some of the leaders, once they were provided with a chance to explore EPS and ask questions about it, could see that the new process might deliver benefits. Like their U.S. counterparts, the Canadian union leaders also saw that management getting closer to the ground through discussions with employees was not a bad thing. A good deal of the resistance began to crumble.

Talking Frankly

The sticking point in every conversation with union leaders was always their conviction that EPS was just another disciplinary tactic. Every conversation went pretty much the same way.

"The company is not going to use it for discipline."

"Then why do it?"

"Because we want to recognize good performance."

The disbelief didn't waver. It was too much a reversal of management practice, where the only reason to have a private conversation was to yell at staff. The only thing to do was to be frank, and frame it bluntly.

"Look, we know the five to ten per cent of poor performers. They're already on our radar. We don't need to design EPS to get them. We've already got them."

That frankness did the trick. They might remain opposed philosophically to performance reviews, but they no longer thought it was about discipline.

The solution to the impasse was to craft a letter which confirmed that EPS was not going to be used for discipline. Once the letter was approved and in the hands of the unions, the grievances disappeared. It had been a bit of a rocky road, but it was resolved finally.

A Hard Lesson Learned

It is not a good idea to drop a change initiative without warning people who are gathered in a group setting. They only have to look around the room to find allies in resistance. Those allies reinforce their outrage and opposition becomes entrenched. When it comes to a major change initiative, it's better to consult separately with the key opinion leaders.

CHAPTER 10

KEEPING SCORE

While the issues with the unions were being resolved, the project continued. First on the team's mind was how to record the results of the performance evaluation sessions. A "scorecard" had been proposed, and getting it right was central to the design of the EPS process. It would be the document handed to employees, and they would keep it as a record of the conversation in the session. It had to look good, and it had to be clear and meaningful for both the supervisor and the employee.

There was agreement that the scorecard had to look good and be clear. There was also agreement that it had to feature defined performance criteria, a set of measurements and a rating system. It took a while to get agreement on all of these factors. Maybe because it was going to be the most tangible part of the process, or maybe because there were so many possible options, precious time was spent spinning wheels.

Gradually, the options for the scorecard were narrowed and choices were made. One of those choices was an early decision that the EPS process was going to be transparent. What was said to the employees, what the scorecard said and what was put in the employee's files would all match exactly. There were going to be no hidden comments or observations secretly held in anyone's file. EPS was going to be a landmine-free zone.

That decision threw light on the path to other decisions. If it was going to be transparent, then the easiest way to go was to keep it as simple as possible. The mantra became "make it simple". The plan was that the EPS scorecard could be printed by the supervisors in their offices. It would have all of the performance objectives on it, along with the relevant measurements, supplied by the data system. Then away the supervisors could go to do the session once they added the performance ratings.

Selecting the Performance Criteria

EPS was an opportunity to push the Five Business Principles down into the organization, so there was no question that they would be the central performance criteria on the scorecard. The question was how to make them meaningful and relevant to the jobs of the unionized employees.

How could a Principle, such as Customer Service, be made meaningful for employees? There would be some kind of relationship to everyone's job in the company, but it might be indirect and not very clear to the individual. The hope was that having the Business Principles on every scorecard would help bring clarity to the employees about those relationships and keep them top of mind.

Defining Measurements

How the performance of an employee would be measured against the Business Principles would depend on what function the employee worked in, and what were their jobs. The second issue was how to get the measurements as close to the individual as possible. Realistically, there was not going to be individual data for all of the measures. Group data would have to be the main source of measurement, at least in the beginning. While not the perfect solution, it would give individuals a sense of how their work group was meeting objectives. When it was possible, individual data would be added to the scorecard.

To make sure that the measures were the right ones, input was needed from the operations side. They knew how to connect the dots between the Business Principles and the relevant group and individual measurements. Then the team would work out how to get the actual data.

For the People Count principle, it was decided that there would be no measurement attempts at all. Instead, this category became an opportunity for the supervisors to shift gear and redirect the conversation. Rather than continue to tell individual employees about their ratings, the supervisors would ask for feedback on how they could help their people. There was a hope that the question "How can I help you do your job better?" would lead to a dialogue.

Rating Wars

The rating system is one of the keys to success in designing a performance evaluation process. It is also one of the tricky components. What makes it tricky is that it has to be clear and understood by two different groups: the ones who do the ratings and the ones who receive them.

The Performance Curve

One of the early objections from the union leaders was that every unionized employee would be forced onto a bell curve with EPS. What they failed to appreciate was that while a bell curve is the most likely result when a general population is being measured, the performance curve changes shape when used with a business population. A business population is "pre-selected." People are screened before hiring, and continue to be screened over time by virtue of performing well enough to stay employed. As a result, the performance curve for a business population skews to the right and loses the shape of a traditional bell.

There are scales in a variety of performance evaluation systems which yield five to nine different ratings. The problem with them is that few people can use them to arrive at an accurate rating. The more ratings a system has, the finer the distinction that must be made between levels of performance. It seemed unlikely that the supervisors, new to performance evaluation, would be able to make those distinctions.

The mantra of "make it simple" dictated a cleaner choice. The idea grew that a four-point rating system would be used. A rating of four would be for an individual with outstanding performance, and a three would indicate good performance. A two would stand for average performance, and a one would be for someone who was too new in a job to rate or who had significant development needs.

While the team debated, the SVP spoke up.

"Let's have three ratings. Outstanding, skilled and too new to rate or needs improvement."

The project team came back in strong disagreement. Only three choices seemed too narrow. The arguments escalated, but eventually the project team saw the sense of the idea. Three ratings would be simple, and make it easy for the supervisors to distinguish between them.

Paul says, "It turned out to be the right thing to do. It made sense to people, and that language has become part of the culture. Eventually, the management performance system adopted the same categories."

Prototype Development

Once the performance criteria, defined measurements and the rating scale were chosen, attention turned to the development of a prototype scorecard. Without a budget to have a professional graphic artist to design it, the team exercised their creativity and took various shots at it.

The earliest attempts didn't meet with much favour. Then, one person simply took initiative, sat down and produced the format. Her design incorporated everything that was needed for the scorecard. On the right side of the page sat the Five Business Principles. In the middle was space for group ratings, and on the right side could be placed individual ratings when they were available.

A simple sweep of the eye could take in all of the relevant information, both across and down the page for the first four Business Principles. The People Count principle started off the second page, which signaled a planned shift in the EPS conversation. Then there were more boxes for inserting the overall rating, any career aspirations and additional comments from either party in the discussion.

You Can Have Anything You Like, But It Looks Like This

It wasn't long before input was received about the scorecard from the field. In keeping with the theme of "make it simple", the original plan was to produce a scorecard for each main job category. Maybe six or so scorecards would be done in total for the first year. The field disagreed.

The field's perspective was that while jobs might be sorted into a few different categories, they might have different aspects to them. They wanted scorecards which related to those aspects, and they wanted flexibility in the design. Their concern was that the scorecard had to be relevant.

It was tough to argue with their perspective, simply because it made sense. The team gave in with barely a murmur, in part because it demonstrated the field's interest, and in part because it strengthened the process. Before very little time had gone by, the originally intended six scorecard versions multiplied into over 50 versions. Only the U.S. Division went with one scorecard.

While the team agreed to make different versions of the scorecard, there was no negotiation on the overall design. In the end, the field was told that they could have any variation that they wanted, as long as it followed the same design for the scorecard. There was neither the time, nor more importantly, the patience, for changing the basic design of the scorecard to suit each division.

I Want It in Colour

Paul had been thinking about the scorecard. It was looking good, but for him it lacked one element. He believed that having it in colour, rather than black and white, would make it more distinctive. It was what an employee would keep from the EPS session, and it needed to be memorable.

"I want it in colour. Let's print it in colour," said Paul to Cathy and Sara.

"No. It can't be done in colour," came the polite response.

"I want it in colour."

"We want the supervisors to be able to print out the Scorecard in their office, right? There aren't very many colour printers in the field. All they can print it in is black and white."

"I want it in colour."

"Don't be an idiot."

Wisely, Paul decided to retreat. He would let some time go by before he returned to this particular issue. It would give him a chance to think up some new and more convincing arguments. It was important not to let it go, but he who survives a dispute, gets to argue it another day.

It was a few weeks before he met with Sara and Cathy again, and was prepared to reargue his case. Before he could, they handed him a new scorecard.

"It's in colour!"

"You were right. It looks better."

It was a very magnanimous response by Cathy and Sara. Having the scorecard in colour meant it had to be printed by HR in head office and then shipped to the field. Printing 18,000 scorecards and getting them in the right hands at the right time was not going to be easy. It was, in fact, going to be torturous, and add to an already heavy workload.

At last, the scorecard was looking good. It had the right performance criteria and measures that would be relevant, a ratings system that supervisors and employees could understand, and enough flexibility to reassure concerns in the field. And, it was in colour. It was that last decision, which broke with the mantra of "make it simple", that would lead to endless trouble.

CHAPTER 11

DEATH BY DATA

The core premise behind any system of performance evaluation is that individuals receive information which lets them understand how their efforts are seen. The data must be accurate and relevant if it is to be meaningful to the person. Should these data conditions not be met, the process fails.

Data may come in an objective form. There may be work statistics kept on how many invoices are checked, how much machinery has been repaired or on-time deliveries have been made. Personal information may be tracked also, such as absences or overtime worked. This is quantitative, hard data, captured in an organization's record keeping.

Qualitative data is soft. It consists of impressions and perceptions, which may or may not be accurate. This data may only be stored in a supervisor's memory, or in rough notes. There could also be commendation or complaint letters, which describe a sample of a person's behavior.

Ideally, a review will focus on the hard data available, but may be distorted by soft information to some degree. It will be woven together to complete a full picture for the individual, and it will carry meaning.

There was a problem, though, with data for EPS. It seems there was not any consistent way of accessing either hard or soft data for all employees.

50 Ways to Store Data

The intent right from the start was not to create any new data. There was no time to do it, and data already in the system was likely to be most accurate and accessible. It was necessary to have statistics that were as close to the individual as possible, and if they weren't available, team numbers could be used. Team numbers were sure to be in the system.

There was a lot of data needed for the scorecards. With the field wanting customized, rather than generic, scorecards, they had to have relevant data which could be taken down as far as possible to the actual job. The challenge was that there were dozens of different jobs.

The company has a ton of data. The problem was it didn't keep that data in only one system, but in multiple systems. The systems didn't all talk to each other, and they didn't talk to HR. Some of the data collection systems were still manual, which meant HR couldn't pick and choose the data to download and put in a new system to support the EPS process.

Immediately, the IT department was brought in to help. IT, being another one of the company's busy groups, couldn't assemble a team for the request. They offered one consultant for the project, and estimated that it would take six months to produce three separate performance scorecards. The budget would be around $600,000, charged back to HR.

There had to be a different way to get it done. While IT pressed for the use of SAP as the platform for EPS, the project couldn't hang in limbo for six months. In six months the rollout had to happen, and it would need multiple scorecards. There was some fast and flexible thinking done in order to support the survival of EPS.

First, HR staff was sent scurrying to identify where the right data was located in the myriad of systems. Then, a contract programmer was hired to create the EPS system, drawing on the nine different systems in use that contained the needed data. It was not going to be easy.

A Running Dog Fight

As Cathy delved into the multitude of data systems, a new surprise was discovered. It wasn't just that the systems didn't talk to each other. The systems didn't even talk the same language.

Take, for example, the effort to get hard data on absenteeism. It was chosen as a measure of productivity, because if an employee isn't on the job, productivity takes a hit. The problem was that every system seemed to define and measure it differently.

On the surface, absenteeism seems simple to measure. The person is there at work, or not. When it comes to documenting absenteeism, though, the systems recorded it differently. In some places, it was recorded as days worked. In other places, it was recorded as days missed. Still other systems recorded vacation days under the heading of absenteeism.

There were other quirks, too. There are rest days, which didn't count as absenteeism, nor were they counted as days worked. There were job changes, and when they happened, attendance didn't get captured always. Depending on the system, and how it measured, there were gaps in expected attendance, but no way to explain them.

Then there was the issue of how to classify absenteeism, depending on whether it was an authorized absence or a personal one. An authorized absence might be the result of a suspension. If there were a lot of suspensions, that might raise questions about how effectively management was doing its job. Those questions could be forestalled by not counting suspensions as absences.

Or it might be that an individual had a need for a day off for personal reasons, asked for it and was given permission. That permission might or might not show up in the record as absenteeism, but there seemed to be a good chance that overtime would be granted to someone else in the work team to cover the absence. The HR team wanted to be sure that what was measured was whether a person was at work, not a supervisor's covert reward system.

By the time the right questions had been asked, a two page document was assembled which showed all of the different ways in which absenteeism was defined. Nor were some of answers easy to get. It was a running dog fight, as managers wanted to protect their "system", which in turn protected their self-interests.

To have a consistent measure of absenteeism, it had to created. It became the percentage of days in which an individual showed up and was available for work.

The Solace of Aspirin

There was some trouble getting other data as well. Managers are protective of information and data. Some of it was given out routinely, so there was no hesitation in that case. Other numbers were internal, and people were territorial about it, which was another hurdle to jump. Then all of the data collected from various sources had to be transposed into the newly developed EPS system.

There wasn't anything glamorous about it. It was just pure pain. If a system recorded vacation days under absenteeism, those days had to be taken out to get a correct tally for EPS. If the system measured days worked, then to find the absenteeism figure, days on the job had to be subtracted from the total numbers of work days in that location.

The company also has a host of collective agreements. They have different definitions for work days, authorized leaves and absenteeism, which added to the headache.

To Be or Not to Be Qualitative

Hard data was necessary for EPS, and with enough battling, it was achieved. It also would have been helpful to create opportunities for supervisors to add their impressions into the feedback for employees. It might be soft data, but it would be useful for people to hear things like "I remember when you went the extra mile when we were shorthanded," or "Your idea about how to fix the customer's problem worked perfectly."

Soft data makes people realize that their behavior is noticed and defined, and that it is appreciated. In the day-to-day melee of operations, a supervisor might have time to say "Good job", but not have the time to say why it was a job well done. Explaining the "why" gives people more chances to know what they are doing right, and more chance to shape their behavior in a desired direction. It helps to make the feedback very individual.

However, it quickly became apparent that there were going to be some shortfalls on soft data. Some supervisors didn't work closely with people, so they wouldn't have many impressions to add. Supervisors would be encouraged to add comments when they could, but not every employee could get soft data on the first round of EPS.

Staying Pragmatic

A hard look at the data issues made it quite clear that the EPS project was going to require adaptation to circumstances and a pragmatic mindset. The rule of "Create No New Data" had to be broken, but that was for hard data and only for absenteeism. There was no opportunity to take any extra steps to get soft data.

The belief was that over time the supervisors would get comfortable with EPS and would see its value. At that point, they would realize that knowing more about an individual's track record on the job would help them to do the reviews. Then they would have a good incentive to be more observant and thoughtful about their people's performance. They would learn for themselves to store soft data to feed into EPS.

It was time to move forward to the next step.

CHAPTER 12

THEY DON'T NEED TRAINING

The company had spent time and money to provide all management ranks with ABC training. When the question arose about training for first-line supervisors as part of the project, to help them with performance conversations, the SVP, HR, thought about the ABC training that had been done. It seemed an unnecessary waste of time and money to repeat aspects of that training.

His reply to the team was, "They don't need training."

Unanimously, the project team replied, "Yes, they do need training. They absolutely need training. It's not a nice-to-have, it's a must-have to make the project work."

Despite repeated "nos", the issue was revisited three times before the team got the answer they wanted. "Okay, it's your project. Do it your way."

Implicit in those words was "You'd better be right about this", but the team had thought carefully about the question of training and was certain that it was needed. While most of the supervisors had received ABC training, not everyone had been reached, and some still had only a hazy understanding of it. Good feedback skills would be needed for EPS. It was not just another piece of process being introduced into the company: EPS was culture change.

Culture change involves a chain reaction. One segment of change leads to another, with the current piece being built on the last one. Get a segment wrong, and it damages what has preceded it in the chain, and puts future steps at risk. The training for first-line supervisors would be risk management insurance to keep the culture change chain from being broken.

First-line supervisors gave feedback every day on the job. But they used their feedback skills to make sure that they were heard by employees. Now, they were going to have to learn how to listen to employees in a feedback session. That shift in emphasis is a major evolution with feedback, and the supervisors would need support to make it happen. With these needs in mind, Sara took on the design of the training plan.

What Is the End Game?

At the end of the day, EPS needed to be a "wow" experience for employees. For it to be successful in year one, employees needed to feel that their contributions were recognized and appreciated. They needed to see how their work connected with the company's Business Principles, and how their individual contributions fit in with larger goals. The goal was for them to be happy about the process and see the value of EPS.

There was a good chance that employees would be wary and dubious about EPS. With rumours spreading about it, there might be a fair number of people who arrive at their EPS session with either a confused or negative outlook. Beyond that consideration, it was a new experience for employees, so people were likely to be a little nervous about it.

Time and resources were too short to train employees in how to conduct themselves in a performance review, even though how they felt about the EPS process was the end game. To get the "wow" experience, the only option was to train their supervisors. A second reason for training was to build the skill set of the supervisors.

A strong aspect of the culture in the company was that no one talked to employees about performance unless there was a problem. For EPS to work, that mindset would need to be changed. The training would help to start breaking the habit of not talking about performance.

Building the Skill Set for Supervisors

The first part of training is always about the "why". Supervisors had to understand why EPS was important, and how it fit in the context of the ABC training they had already received. They had to come to the realization that it was part of the evolution of the company's culture change journey. EPS was going to be a critical ingredient for the company in building an engaged work force. That part of the training would be teaching and talking, but it's not where the most emphasis would be placed.

To build the supervisors' skill sets, and to get to the "wow" experience for employees, the emphasis in training needed to be on how the supervisors would do the EPS sessions. The decision was made to design the training as learning sessions. A facilitator would lead the participants, and by designing the sessions to be interactive, allow the supervisors to teach themselves.

People learn best when they can build on what they already know, and the ABC training had given the majority of supervisors some basic feedback skills. That previous training had been consolidated in the field through their day-to-day activities.

Now, they would have an opportunity to use these skills in a different way, by building on them and pushing them further.

Part of the training design was a basic review of what they already knew. It was made interactive by encouraging the participants to share their experiences in giving feedback. By eliciting success statements about giving feedback, the confidence level of the supervisors would rise that they could tackle another way to use feedback.

Adults benefit from a chance to practice new skills as they acquire an understanding of their mechanics. As part of the training design, there would be role playing, so they could feel what it would be like and get comfortable with the idea of feedback in the context of performance reviews. Questions would inevitably come up about potential issues in the reviews, and the training design was to throw these questions back at the participants to answer.

Post-Training Support

Post-training support is a vital part of transferring learning to the job. The learning sessions by themselves were just the first step in the training plan for the supervisors. Equally necessary was to plan how to support them when they encountered the reality of doing EPS in the field. Ideally, they could step right up and do it. In reality, whenever people tackle a new process, the more they are supported the more likely they can do it correctly.

The post-training support for EPS would come in three forms:

The Reference Guide

A reference guide was provided to give supervisors answers to questions that had not been covered in the learning sessions. Paper documentation is quick to access, and the supervisors were accustomed to using it.

Getting the Supervisors' Managers Involved

The first-line supervisors' managers had a role to play in the support system. They were encouraged to hold team meetings, and bring up questions or problems about EPS. This format also gave them a chance to talk about all of the employees, and get a common understanding of how to rank them. The outcome would be more consistency in how the EPS sessions were approached, and the meetings would provide some buddy support for the supervisors.

Internal coaches

The third piece would be to offer the services of an internal coach. Participants had names and numbers to call if they hit a problem or had a question. They could talk it through quickly, which would help to keep them from getting stalled.

Finally, EPS would be an annual event. Supervisors would be measured on their completion of performance reviews. Rewards would be put in place to help them change their behavior and maintain it.

Making Behavior Change Stick

There is often a lot of grumbling in the business world that training doesn't work. Managers count up the time it takes for training, add in the cost, and complain that behavior stays the same once people are back in the work setting.

Let's say that you are not satisfied with how your team functions. You engage a facilitator to do team building, but back at the office, your team's behavior hasn't changed. They're still hogging resources, stealing credit and casting blame, and generally being intensely competitive with one another.

Training is an antecedent, and just one of the signals for behavior change. Behavior changes when the rewards change. If you want your team to be co-operative, you have to reward co-operative behavior. Don't blame the training. Look in the mirror.

Linking from Top to Bottom

The executives and senior managers had bought into EPS, and were giving it their backing. They kept the communication flowing in order to keep focus on this project. It was reaching the middle that was the problem.

The Murky Middle

The company, depending on where you sit in the organization, has six to seven layers from top to bottom. Getting a consistent, clear message through those layers can be difficult. It seems to be in the middle layers where it gets lost, and where a good number of change initiatives have the highest risk of death. One of the lessons learned from change is that if you can't figure out how to link the top to the bottom so everyone is on message, then forget it. It won't work. Don't even bother. You need a plan.

Part of the solution was to encourage the senior operating people to make EPS a regular part of the agenda in scheduled meetings. For example, the head of the U.S. Division had it on the agenda for every meeting. By asking consistently how many sessions had been done, how many more to do, where the roadblocks were and who needed a word in their ear, it stayed alive and urgent for the middle management ranks.

Another part of the solution was to engage the regional HR Managers in the process beyond delivering the training. They would encourage the managers of the supervisors to show up for the training sessions, either to be participants or to answer questions. The presence of their bosses would give the right signal to the supervisors that the EPS initiative was important and a priority.

Make It Simple

Once the supervisors started the actual EPS sessions, it was important that they didn't waste energy or lose focus. Their time was at a premium, so the process needed to be as smooth and flawless as possible. It was going to be absolutely necessary to keep the bureaucracy to a minimum, and not let the supervisors have to work through a paper maze or be distracted by the background mechanics of the process.

To make it easy, the plan was to provide every supervisor with easy access to all the information they needed to conduct the EPS session. The scorecard would be sent to them, and then they could add the performance ratings and just walk into their scheduled meetings.

Final Preparation

In concert with the senior operations managers, there was a negotiation over how much time was available for training the supervisors. HR wanted a full day; operations wanted a half day. It was sawed off at six hours.

Next was adding the actual content to the training framework. The learning modules were based on HR's estimate of the supervisors' needs. In particular, it was believed that they would benefit from a refresher course in how to give feedback. Within the context of performance management, they needed to learn how to manage people's responses and answer questions.

With the prototype scorecards ready, and the pilots scheduled, it was time to go to the next step. The pilots would provide feedback to help fine-tune the training process and dictate any changes necessary. Quickly after that step would be the mass production of training and EPS materials for the sessions scheduled to rollout in the following months.

In high spirits, the team set off to start the pilots. It's where reality was encountered, and reality bit back.

CHAPTER 13

THROWING LIGHT INTO DARK CORNERS

While running a pilot of the training process might seem like a luxury given the short timelines, the team saw it as a necessity. Feedback from the pilots would help to strengthen the material and see if anything had been overlooked. HR wasn't betting the company on EPS, but there was a high imaginary wager on it. The pilots would hedge the bet.

The pilots were scheduled for three sites: Accounting in Toronto; the Northwest's Division yard in Vancouver; and the U.S. Division's Michigan site. All three would be done in March of 2006, which gave a month to make adjustments and start production for the full rollout.

All of the content had been designed to enable the first-line supervisors to meet certain objectives in EPS sessions. In the actual sessions, they needed to:

- Understand how to prepare for the sessions;
- Be able to explain the EPS process, the reason for its implementation and the probable benefits for the employee, the supervisor and the company;
- Use their communication skills in providing relevant feedback on performance measures, and present the scorecard;

- Listen and respond to comments or questions;
- Be able to handle a range of possible reactions from employees;
- Take note of suggestions or ideas from employees;
- Confirm that the employee understood the feedback; and
- Close the session with comments on any next steps.

The objectives for the supervisors seemed to be reasonable and achievable, and the content of the training was wrapped around supporting these behaviors.

The First Whammy

The supervisors participating in the sessions had a few questions that had not been anticipated. The dialogue went something like this interchange.

Supervisor: "Who will I do the sessions with?"

Facilitator: "Your direct reports."

Supervisor: "Who are my direct reports?"

Facilitator: "The people you direct on a day-to-day basis."

Supervisor: "But I don't see all of the people in my area. I never talk to some of them. How do I know which ones are my direct reports?"

Facilitator: "Don't you know?"

Supervisor: "No."

It was an "uh-oh" moment. How could any of the supervisors not know who reported to them? And it wasn't just one person, it was quite a few of them, and that was happening just during the pilots. The team needed to take a close look at this issue and get a handle on it before the rollout.

Like most accidents, this one had multiple causes, all threatening to come together at exactly the wrong moment. Some of the field supervisors managed employees in different geographic locations, which meant they didn't see them or talk to them on a regular basis. On the other hand, some supervisors worked in the same location with their employees, and still rarely saw or talked to them.

Take for example the scheduling of drivers. Supervisors in logistics are in charge of making sure that the right products for customers get picked up or delivered at the right time. The unionized drivers, though, keep moving between customers' plants and their destinations, and may be on the road for days. With hundreds of employees, and everyone on shift work, the supervisors see route documentation more than they see actual people.

Also, the supervisors schedule the needed drivers from a paper roster, and a call centre then connects with the employees and gives them their work assignments. If the employee is not available for some reason, the call centre will keep contacting people until there are sufficient drivers. The supervisors probably wouldn't know about such substitutions, only that the loads were being moved according to schedule.

There was a scramble for a solution. The hope was that this information would turn up on SAP, which documented all of the reporting relationships. Except, as it was discovered, that system stopped above the first-line supervisors. That left HR making calls to track and document who reported to who, so first-line supervisors could be provided with a list of the employees with whom they would be doing EPS.

The Second Whammy

There was another surprise in the pilots.

Facilitator: "You can see on the scorecard that there are measures for activities which are important in the job. It is against these measures that you will provide feedback to your people based on their performance."

Supervisor: "On this scorecard, it says the measurement is delivery compliance. What's delivery compliance?"

Facilitator: "The measurement will be the percentage of time that the goal for delivery compliance was met."

Supervisor: "Okay, but what's delivery compliance?"

Facilitator: "It's connected to the service plan agreement with customers. Delivery plan compliance is the measurement for how well a given service plan with customers is met."

Supervisor: "I never heard of it before."

How could this happen? How could the supervisors not know, down to the last detail, these performance measures? Was it really possible they didn't know?

Well, as the team discovered, it was all too possible. Measures of overall performance are set at the corporate level. These measures were ones that the senior people in operations, in this example, believed were crucial to getting the right business results, and they had fed them into EPS. All of the measures related to the Business Principles, in this case the principle of Customer Service.

It was obvious that there were some crucial links missing here, and it wasn't a trivial issue. If the supervisors didn't have a good understanding of the measures, how could they influence them? How could they direct their people to improve results? If the goal for delivery compliance was at 95%, and your location was at 90%, an improvement was needed. You couldn't do it, though, if you didn't know the measure existed.

The Triple Whammy

The surprises from the pilots weren't finished.

Facilitator: "You may find out during the session, based on the conversation with your employee, that he or she may be lacking knowledge or training. What would be a good response to that need on your part?"

Supervisor: "Tell them, I guess, to go find the information they need."

Facilitator: "How could you direct them to the right resources?"

Supervisor: "Ask them to call HR, I suppose."

Facilitator: "Would you consider coaching them? Coaching them could be a next step agreed upon at the end of the EPS session."

Supervisor: "Coaching isn't my job."

This one was a shock. It's when it was discovered that how the supervisors defined their jobs, and how HR assumed that they defined their jobs, was quite different. From the supervisors' point of view, their job was to get assigned work activities completed. While they did it by giving tasks to employees, the focus of the supervisors was on completion of the work, not people.

If supervisors wanted to know if a task had been completed, they checked their reports. The company has great systems that captured this information. What the system does not capture is how well the task is done, or if the person doing it has all the right training and information. Senior management's assumption was that the supervisors were monitoring people's performance and providing support through coaching or training. The supervisors didn't see working with individual employees as part of their job.

Getting Over It

It was from these conversations with the supervisors in the pilot training sessions that these issues were discovered. Without the training and the pilots to reveal these problems, EPS might have been doomed.

The team had to rethink in a hurry. The fundamentals of the training plan were sound, and could be kept in place. The actual content of the training and some of the emphasis in delivering it would be shifted.

From being focused solely on EPS, the training would broaden and become a larger educational experience for the supervisors. Measurements would be defined so that the supervisors weren't caught short by not knowing what they meant or how they applied to their area of responsibility. HR would discover and supply the names of their direct reports. The definition of the supervisory job would be broadened, and they would receive some training help on how to coach.

Looking back, you could say that these discoveries, despite being a surprise at the time, were serendipitous. They had the potential to do some serious damage to the organization, as long as they remained hidden in dark corners. By throwing a spotlight on them, remedies could be found.

CHAPTER 14

THE BACK STORY

How did the situation occur where first-line supervisors didn't realize that people were as much as part of their jobs as tasks? It happened pretty much the same way as in other large organizations. People get promoted from the front ranks when they are good at their jobs. The underlying assumption is that if a person is good at what they do today, they'll be good in a more senior role.

It's simple really. The head of sales will put the top sales person on the short list for the first opening in sales management. If you're the whiz kid in marketing, someone will be thinking of you as a marketing manager. If you're in accounting, and can make numbers dance and tell interesting stories, your next career stop is likely going to be a management role in finance.

In the company, the best accounting clerk, the best mechanic or the best driver will be turned into supervisors. The basic qualifications needed are people who are good at doing what they're doing, are reliable and make nice with their boss. It helps if they have expressed some interest in management, but it's not really necessary.

It's a time honoured tradition to promote someone who is good at their job, and expect that they'll learn along the way about how to lead. Only that learning doesn't always happen.

It's the reason there were supervisors in the company who didn't know that leading people was included in their responsibilities.

In a Hard Place

Supervisors have one of the toughest jobs in management. They're the meat in the sandwich, packed in between upper levels of management and front-line employees. Both sides push and pull at them, often wanting outcomes that are contradictory. If supervisors take a hard management line, they'll make their people unhappy. If they are soft with people, their bosses will grumble that they're letting people get away with things. Finding the right balance, where both bosses and unionized employees can be managed effectively, is hard.

Organizationally, the supervisor's job is to make sure that the right things happen on a day-to-day basis. They have to get the tasks done, and get them done on time. Caught up in daily deadlines, they're often too busy to pay close attention to people unless something goes wrong. Making a mistake is a sure way to get their attention.

Supervisors are the first line of defense with operational mistakes. They have to be fixed quickly, because they tend to reverberate up the line and get noticed. If you're a supervisor, the last thing you want is your manager, or worse your manager's boss, on the line about an urgent problem. Supervisors are likely to deal with issues in the most direct way. Which means that for most unionized employees at the company, being told that your supervisor wants to see you in his or her office is not good news. You're in trouble. You may not know exactly what is that you have done wrong, but you can be certain that the conversation is going to be one-way and unpleasant.

The inherent tensions in the supervisory job were going to be part and parcel of the training provided to the supervisors to do EPS. They were going to have to learn how to have conversations that centred on the person, not the task. They had to realize that coaching and supporting their people was part of the job. To move forward, some of them were going to have to unlearn what they had learned from experience.

Letting Experience Be the Teacher

Once in the supervisor's job, people would probably get some advice from their boss and, in recent years, some training. For many supervisors, though, most of the training in the past had been learning through experience. If you believed that you had a good boss, chances are that you would imitate that boss. If you had a bad boss, you might decide it would be a good idea to do the exact opposite of what that person did.

Basically, supervisors were left to look around them and decide who was a successful manager in the organization and then model that person's behavior. The problem was that the definition of success in the company had changed a good deal over the years. At one time, success was all about not making waves and keeping your head down. If you had been a supervisor for a long time, management by abdication was likely your original model.

After the IPO, the model changed. Success came from the manager who got things done and behaved in a way that contributed to profitability. There were lots of stories in the newspapers about the company's emergence as a profit engine, and internally there was pressure to get better and better results. As a supervisor, you could look around the company and see which managers above you got recognized and rewarded for those results.

If you wanted to please and get ahead, you would continue the same behavior that helped to achieve good results. Such a move, however, was no guarantee that you were learning to be an effective manager, only that you were getting good short-term results. You might be doing some things very wrong in the name of getting results and not know the difference. Nor would your boss necessarily be in a hurry to set you straight. Without that feedback, you'd become convinced you were behaving the right way.

Now, the need was to move managers beyond that model of "results first" to a new level. They needed to engage people in their work, and let go of the command and control model. Certainly, there were managers in the company who had reached this level, but they were not yet the bulk of management personnel. Supervisors might not have seen too many of them in action. That lack of leadership meant that many of them had not had the chance to learn how to imitate the model of a Q4 manager who could balance results with good people leadership.

Experience may be the best teacher, if what's being imitated is the best behavior. When it's not, experience can be a very scary teacher.

DCOM

Some of these new learning needs for supervisors had been tackled with the ABC and Q4 training. It takes a while, though, to make sure everyone has the training. It takes even longer to make sure that people get appropriate consequences to consolidate their changed behaviors. Obviously, there were still supervisors who were all over the place in terms of their management competency.

A decision was made to add another element to the supervisory training for EPS. The DCOM model had been developed to support the Q4 training from CLG. It was a short, clear way for supervisors to picture in their heads how to approach being a leader of people.

Direction (D)

The leader who gives direction successfully provides people with a clear understanding of what is to be done and why it is important. This direction establishes what the expected outcome will be, what standard of quality is required and assigns specific responsibility for tasks. If there is a need to shift priorities, the leader will promptly communicate this change.

Competence (C)

Leaders have to insure that people are able to perform their assigned tasks successfully. It's the leader's responsibility to accurately assess the degree of skill and knowledge an individual employee has to complete a task, and to support that person through coaching and new learning. There are strong components of feedback and listening in this part of the model, and patience on the part of the manager as people make the inevitable mistakes involved in learning.

Opportunity (O)

It's the leader's job to make sure that people have all the tools and resources necessary to do the work that has been assigned. It may mean that the leader has to remove barriers or influence others to gain co-operation, as well as supply information, funding or sufficient timelines.

Motivation (M)

Leaders who need people to follow them have to develop trust with their employees and demonstrate confidence in them. This behavior involves not just giving feedback, but also being receptive to it and the ideas of others. There is a strong emphasis on rewarding and recognizing appropriate behavior, providing encouragement and celebrating successes.

The DCOM model was intended to help supervisors put together all of the pieces from the ABC and Q4 training that they needed to lead people. It was putting a stake in the ground and saying, "Yes, you are responsible for your people. You need to get results, and the best way to get them is through people."

The EPS sessions were also going to bring some of these pieces together. For the first time, supervisors were going to focus the conversation on what employees did right. They were going to listen to their ideas for improvement and career wishes. They were going to offer support for development. The revised training plan would help them be comfortable in facing this new task.

Now, it was time for the rollout.

CHAPTER 15

A LITTLE LOGISTICAL MAYHEM

The logistics of the rollout were formidable. There were 18,000 unionized employees to reach, in two countries and two languages, and more micro-cultures than you could count. Before they could have their EPS sessions, 1,200 supervisors had to be trained. Before the rollout of the 165 training sessions for supervisors could be started, the train-the-trainer sessions had to take place. There were only eight months in which to accomplish this agenda.

The plan was simple, even if executing it was complicated. Unlike the usual practice of having performance reviews done in the same time period across an organization, EPS was going to be a staggered process. The training and subsequent EPS sessions would rollout in waves one after the other in each of the three divisions across the eight months.

Within each division, as training for the supervisors took place, the graduates would start almost immediately on the EPS sessions with their people. The shorter the time gap, the more likely they would retain what they had learned in the sessions and be able to put it into practice. It was known which supervisors were in which training sessions, so HR knew which scorecards were needed. The trick was going to be to get them there on time.

Just to complicate things a little further, nothing about EPS was yet finalized totally. There wasn't the luxury of making sure that every aspect of it was perfect before it was launched formally. It was time to sink or swim.

A Moving Target

The pilots provided some good lessons. As more feedback was received from each pilot, the training was changed in approach in order to correspond to the needs expressed. Training aids and material for the participants were produced on the fly, and then changed as a new group went through the next pilot.

EPS was an entirely new experience for the supervisors, and it became apparent quickly that they needed help in explaining it. The supervisors first had to understand it, and then be comfortable with explaining it to their people. Cathy, who sat in on all the pilots, listened closely to the role plays. She captured the best descriptions of EPS from them, and that script, in the words of the supervisors, became part of the training.

While normally the end of the pilots would have marked the point where the training was crystallized, Sara and Cathy were not satisfied entirely with it yet. Continuous upgrading of the training process and materials went on until about the tenth session in the actual rollout.

Training the Trainers

For the first time, the company used its own people to do most of the training in the field. Thirty-one Human Resources Managers underwent the train-the-trainer sessions, drawn from across all the divisions. The sessions were led by Sara and Cathy. Also included in this training were the ABC coaches within the company, who tended to be business leaders. They would be the primary delivers of the training in the U.S., as the logistical process there was different.

There was an important message to deliver to the prospective trainers. They had to master the process and the material, but they also had to stay adaptable. Some participants had more ABC training than others; some participants had better management skills in general. Some supervisors had easy access to their people; others had people spread across a wide territory which added complexity to the logistics of the rollout. The trainers would need to tailor their approach and materials depending upon the audience.

I Want A CD

As the training finally got more or less set, Paul decided that the supervisors would benefit from having a CD of the session. They could refer to it any time that they wanted, and the material would remain clear to them.

"No way," said Cathy and Sara. "There's no budget for it."

"I want a CD. It's a good thing." Paul had a dozen reasons to support his request.

"You're not going to get it." Once again, heels were dug in, and the discussion was closed.

A few weeks later, Paul was presented with the CD. Cathy and Sara did their research, found the right supplier and managed the budget. It was one of the lessons from EPS. Don't waste time saying why something can't be done; put energy into finding a way to do it.

Even after the CD was burned, the HRM trainers were warned that the training would keep changing. They couldn't just memorize the material, and deliver it by rote. It was a little bit like asking them to jump out of an airplane without being sure exactly when their parachutes would open. To avoid hitting the ground with an unwelcome thump, they had to learn to dance in mid-air. They rose to the challenge well, and their enthusiasm helped immensely with the successful delivery of the training for the supervisors.

Producing the Scorecards

The decision to produce the EPS scorecards in colour was the right one to support the new process, but proved to be a minefield for Cathy and her project team. There were few colour printers in the field, so the supervisors couldn't download the data they needed and print the scorecards in their offices before the EPS sessions. All of the scorecards would have to be produced by HR. The timing was going to be tight.

There were 18,000 Scorecards needed. They had to be sent across the U.S. and Canada, and the delivery was going to be just-in-time. To simplify the delivery logistics, the decision was made to send them to main regional offices. From there, they would be delivered to the specific sites.

Of course, when you're sending out 18,000 scorecards, you're just asking for trouble. Cathy kept hearing the same refrain.

"We need the scorecards."

"They've been shipped."

"They're not here!"

Where were they? Well, they were stacked in boxes under someone's desk, or leaning against the wall in a heap of cartons, or put in a storage room so that "everybody knows where there are." The HR team wondered if miniature GPS tracking devices could be put into the cartons, so people could follow a beeping sound to them. It was an annoying problem, but it paled in comparison to the feat of producing the scorecards.

It was true that HR had a colour printer in head office. It did not, however, have an automatic stapling feature. The scorecard package included four pages, which needed to be stapled. Without automatic stapling, it had to be done by hand. The two page individual scorecard, a sheet explaining the measurements and an information piece for employees on updating their personal information on file went into the blue folders to be delivered to the supervisors.

It all added up to stapling 76,000 pieces of paper. By hand.

Blue Folder Parties

The EPS team needed volunteers to provide 18,000 folders to the supervisors. To the team's delight, some suppliers came in to help, and people were kidnapped in the halls, too. Light work was made of it by providing snacks and music, and commandeering boardrooms where everyone could work, but also talk and laugh. Those blue folder parties carry fond memories. Not just because the task got done, but because they let EPS be delivered.

As time went on, the process settled down. It's one part of the project, though, that no one is in a hurry to relive.

Getting It Right and Wrong

Before the scorecards could be shipped, the right ones had to be produced for each employee. At this point, there were over 50 different versions of the scorecard, not the half dozen or so envisioned originally. The production process started with sending the employees' pin numbers into HR, which are their company identification for record-keeping purposes. The pin numbers would identify which version of the scorecard to produce and ship.

The trouble was that the pin list was not entirely accurate. So a scorecard would be sent out, only to be identified as the wrong one, and a new one needed to be produced and sent pronto.

Then there was the further problem of making the right decision about what data to include on a scorecard. There are three divisions, and each is organized somewhat differently. Some measures for the scorecards were national, but some could be divisional or right down to a local zone. So which to produce? No one was specifying exactly what they wanted, so some of the decisions made by HR were wrong. There would be a scramble to produce the right data that was needed.

Then there was one other little problem that cropped up occasionally. The company covers an incredible amount of geographic territory. When you're sitting in head office, it turns out you don't know where every field location is. Sometimes the question would have to be asked, "Where exactly is Smithtown?" It was somewhat embarrassing to be getting geography lessons from the field.

There was also a mental image of the manager requesting the scorecards. Would it be with delight or horror as that person asked silently, "Head office doesn't know where we are?"

No Choice in the Matter

Despite these problems, the team persevered. What added to the urgency was the fact that the EPS sessions couldn't be done without the scorecards. It was one thing to ask the trainers to dance with a generic scorecard in training the supervisors; it was another one entirely to ask the supervisors to do it in the EPS sessions.

The supervisors had to have the right scorecard at the right time. Given the logistical hurdles that had to be jumped, the initial prediction that only 250 scorecards could be produced each week was going to fall far short of what was necessary. At that rate, it was going to take 18 months to finish EPS.

It's true what is said about necessity being the mother of invention. Ways to jump and dodge hurdles were invented, and the production rate soared to a 1,000 a week.

A Continuous Feedback Loop

EPS, given its surprise announcement and tight timing, was a first of its kind project within the company. There was no chance to plan for it far in advance or work out all of the kinks before it was implemented. It was a project that depended heavily on inspiration, quick decisions and a rapid pace.

On a daily basis, the team learned what was working and what was not. Information came from observing the training, and from contacting supervisors as they finished their EPS sessions. They were generous in sharing their impressions, both positives and negatives. Superintendents and other managers in the field were helpful also in providing their observations.

The continuous feedback loop allowed the project team to make changes in real time as the project unfolded. The customary project management practice of waiting until the end of a rollout to gather information and then decide how to change the process for the next iteration was abandoned. Instead, constant changes were made as the project unfolded, incorporating the feedback and improving the product.

CHAPTER 16

IN THE FIELD

The moment when EPS would go live in the field had eagerly been awaited. The expectation was that the project was going to deliver good things, and clearly be a change marker for the organization. The basics were all in place. All that was needed was for the supervisors to play their part.

It was also a moment of high anxiety.

Everything the HR team had done up to that moment was an "antecedent." In behavioral terms, that meant that all of the efforts expended so far were only going to account for 20% of the outcome. Certainly, it's critical to get the antecedents right, but they are only the beginning of the story.

The hard work of defining measurements, setting up a system to gather data, creating and producing the scorecards and training every supervisor was going to add up to a small slice of the pie in the end. All of the formal and informal communication that had taken place could influence but would not determine the outcome. It was sobering to realize that this work, which amounted to a tremendous effort, was only a preliminary to the real action.

That real action was going to take place in the field. The behavior of the supervisors — how effectively they delivered the EPS sessions — would determine what the consequences were for the organization. Consequences carry 80% of the weight in determining outcomes.

If unionized employees had good experiences, where they saw that their contributions were recognized and valued, then the outcome would be positive. If they could see no value in the process, than the outcome would be negative.

HR had done all that it could. Now, it was up to the supervisors.

Central Development, Divisional Execution

To the delight of some managers, and to the annoyance of others, the company has a freestyle approach to implementing change projects. HR designed EPS, but how it got executed across the divisions was not by the carbon copy method. Each division, under its Senior Vice-President, could choose how to implement it.

The advantage of this approach is that the Divisions can put their stamp on change, which gives them better ownership. The different methods can be compared, and the ones that work best can be promoted and communicated. The disadvantage is that some mistakes can be made, but at least their impact is limited to one division at a time.

The U.S. Division Takes the Lead

The U.S. Division was far ahead of everybody else with EPS. Right at the start, the SVP and his team sat down and decided how to manage EPS. This division represents a mix of formerly independent ventures, which gives it multiple cultures. Senior management had already worked hard in reaching the supervisors to create a common view. Their efforts had built a platform of trust with the field, and the U.S. Division was quick to get the union leaders to support EPS before the process started.

One of the key decisions made was to include the EPS training with a coaching program from CLG. The need for this training had been identified before EPS came on the horizon. The program had been designed and was ready to implement. Adding the EPS training to it made perfect sense. Coaching was going to be a necessary skill to help close performance gaps, and it was a skill that many supervisors lacked.

The U.S. Division handled EPS in a carefully considered way.

- The senior team had EPS on the agenda for every weekly management meeting, and in every communication piece, and progress was tracked systematically;
- Any barriers that arose were dealt with immediately by selling the positive benefits of EPS and clarifying what supervisors needed to do, which built support for the process;
- Every training session was co-led by a senior leader from the Divisional head office, which signaled to participants that EPS was being taken seriously;
- In each location within the Division, the local management worked as a team before the actual rollout to do a preliminary ranking of their employees and make sure everyone would approach EPS with a similar framework; and
- Heavy coaching and mentoring support was supplied to the supervisors during the rollout.

The U.S. Division led the way on EPS, and had a fairly smooth rollout with its unionized employees. True to form in the company, the success of the rollout was recognized, which provided some encouragement for the other Divisions to try and catch up to it.

Central Division

Central Division had 8,500 unionized employees, spread out from the Maritimes to Manitoba. It was a lot of people and ground to cover, which is perhaps why the initial response from the field there was a simple "Not gonna happen."

The senior management team, however, were determined it was going to happen. There was an enormous selling job to do in a very short time. While there was the normal chorus of "We don't have time for it", the focus was placed on how to do it and the pragmatic problem-solving talents of operations came into play. The senior team kept it on the agenda and dealt with the issues in the division.

- To contain the rumours floating around about EPS, shop stewards were included in early training sessions. Once they realized it really was about feedback and development, they took a neutral stance.
- Supervisors were encouraged to start with those employees with good records, as the sessions would be positive. That decision meant that the first groups of employees had high satisfaction, and built the supervisors' confidence in handling employees more likely to challenge them.

- There were locations in the Central Division with a ratio of one supervisor to 150 employees, and the actual worksites could be some distance apart. That ratio and distance placed a huge burden on those supervisors, and assistant superintendents became partners in getting it done.
- The HRM's, instead of doing the training and then disappearing, took an active role in supporting and coaching the supervisors and became another partner for them.

By December, the Central Division had met their commitment to finish EPS.

Northwest Division

This division had a steep challenge, and because of it, lagged behind the other ones in getting EPS done. The senior team struggled with something that isn't normally thought of as a bad thing to happen. Their business had been growing so fast that the Division was shorthanded. With a critical lack of people, supervisors were, for example, filling in on line jobs as needed. EPS was one more priority for a division under tremendous pressure.

Like Central, the Northwest Division was spread over a huge geographical territory, and there could be one supervisor to over 100 staff. Indeed, in one location, there were 250 people to one supervisor. Just reaching everybody, especially in remote locations, was going to be a challenge by itself.

Supervisors in the Northwest pushed back against EPS, singing the blues even more loudly than the others. They believed that they had conversations with their people every day, and the initiative was going to be a paper exercise with no value. At the same time, they took easily to the training, as their exposure to the ABC's methodology was not that far in the past.

- To deal with the large ratios of employees to supervisors, other managers were pulled in to handle some of the EPS sessions. They were dealing with people that they didn't know at all, but seemed to acquit themselves well.
- The division had full time ABC coaches on board, and they offered a high degree of support for the supervisors.
- Perhaps because of the critical issues in the Northwest which may have been distracting supervisors, the feedback from employees was mixed to a greater degree. Still, most seemed to accept the feedback, and particularly appreciated the opportunity to explore career interests.
- The division was later in finishing EPS, with many supervisors waiting until the very last moment to get it done.
- Despite the initial reservations of the supervisors, people seemed to catch the spirit of EPS, and had ideas how to improve it for the next year.

The Last Part

The last component of the rollout was to implement the EPS process in Head Office functions. That training started in October, and the sessions were finished by the end of the year.

Across the Finish Line

By the end of December, the project was done. The supervisors had risen well to the challenge. The promise to the analysts, that all employees would receive the opportunity for a performance review in 2006, was kept.

CHAPTER 17

FIRST SIGNS OF SPRING

In the northern hemisphere, the arrival of spring is a yearly miracle. The snow melts as the temperature climbs, and the harsh winds of winter change to soft breezes. Trees begin to bud, and the early spring bulbs put forth their blossoms to delight the eye and the spirit. In the depths of winter, spring seems impossible. When it arrives, hope is in the air.

Something very similar happens with projects. Battling against opposition and resistance, you can despair that the project will ever get off the ground. Running a race against a tight timeline, and without enough resources, feels a lot like living under dark winter clouds. Then, while it seems like it will never happen, the results begin to show. Suddenly, it is spring.

Never was spring more welcome. As the staggered rollout of EPS continued across the continent, signs that the new process was working began to be visible. Working, perhaps, even better than had been hoped.

The Impact of Feedback

The rollout for EPS wasn't all that far along when Paul ran into a supervisor who was attending some special training at Head Office. The supervisor had an unsolicited story to tell the other participants in the training session. He had done an EPS session with a union leader, and given that individual a "skilled" rating. With some indignation, the union leader had asked why he was not being rated as outstanding.

The supervisor, perhaps freed by the EPS process, decided to be frank. "Because you're a pain in the ass. You don't make any attempt to get along with people, and that behavior really gets in your way."

The employee, feeling pretty miffed, then went and asked his colleagues for their views. They told him the feedback was all too true. No one, evidently, had ever been straight with him, either supervisors or peers. It wasn't too long before he came back and asked the supervisor for help, so he could learn how to get along with others better.

A Whole Different Buzz

As EPS began to unfold, the participants in the process, both supervisors and employees, began to spread a positive buzz about it. Supervisors told their colleagues how well the employees responded. Some of them were dealing with 30-year veterans, who expressed their appreciation for getting feedback for the first time in their careers. Even some employees who had reputations for being "negative" seemed to accept EPS.

The same positive buzz was coming from employees. People who received a skilled rating were asking supervisors what they could do to get an outstanding rating. How could they improve? What could they do better? Could they have more feedback?

Being a new process, EPS hadn't been all that well understood at first. Most of the unionized employees had been willing to reserve judgement on it, and took a wait-and-see stance. A few had been openly skeptical, and wondered if it was a back door to discipline. As stories from employees began to emerge, EPS was demystified in a good way.

"My boss told me I do a good job. He spent time with me, and listened to me."

"It's the first time anyone said thank you to me for my efforts."

"My boss actually listened to my ideas."

New Learning for the Supervisors

It was obvious that supervisors were learning through EPS. HR began to hear comments from them about the discoveries they made in the sessions.

"I never realized how much Joe knows about customers. He knows more about them than I do."

"Sue had this good idea about how to fix this problem we've been having for a while. She's had the idea for some time, but never wanted to volunteer it. It came out in the EPS conversation."

"John wants to be a supervisor. We've agreed as a first step that he'll be rotated through different jobs in the shop, so he gets a better feel for how everything fits together."

Gradually, it was dawning on the supervisors that they didn't know some of their people very well. By getting to know their people, the supervisors would be in a better position to leverage the employees' strengths. They were beginning to realize that many people had useful ideas to improve productivity, but hadn't brought them out in the past because of lack of encouragement. They were learning that developing people and coaching them was at the heart of their jobs.

The supervisors began to realize also that some of their long held assumptions about unionized workers just weren't true. The employees might all belong to one of the unions, but each one was an individual. They were seeing a wide range of responses to EPS, from highly positive to "Isn't that what you pay me for?" sarcasm. They were realizing that people wanted more from their work than a pay cheque.

And the Race Is On

One employee, who seemed not to like the world very much, surprised people with his response to his EPS session. For the first time, EPS had given employees information about productivity statistics, and he had been doing some private comparisons between his data and the numbers for his teammates. Chatting with his HRM one day, he said, "See that guy over there? He got a better number than me. He's at 85. Well, next year, I'm going to be at 90, and he'll still be at 85. I'm going to be the best."

An Absence of Grievances

HR had formed the impression that some of the union leaders did not have a good opinion of EPS. While the grievances filed when EPS was announced had been dropped, there wasn't much obvious support for the process. They had a guarantee it would not include discipline, but beyond that assurance, no one could predict its exact impact. As a result, most of the union leaders took a neutral stance, where they would neither urge employees to go to the EPS sessions or tell them not to go.

If people didn't like their ratings, and there are always some employees who dispute them, there could very well be trouble.

A complaint from an employee about a rating might push union leaders into filing new grievances.

There was, however, very little push back, and no grievances were filed. Any criticism of EPS was muted, and instead some of the leaders offered positive feedback on it. Some of them told people who complained about their ratings that they should get over it. If they performed better, they'd get a better rating.

"One More Thing"

Not everything was sweetness and light with EPS. Some employees took a strong position against participating in the process, and refused to have conversations about performance with their supervisors. One supervisor, who had become convinced of EPS' value, took an unorthodox approach to countering such resistance.

He arranged to bump into one of his employees who had refused to participate, and struck up what appeared to be a casual conversation. He talked about a few things that the person had done which deserved mention, and thanked him for some of his contributions.

The employee took it all in, listened, and responded with a few suggestions about how to improve things. He thanked his supervisor for the feedback, and reiterated that he was not going to go through EPS.

As the two started to move off to get on with their day, the supervisor said, "Oh, one more thing. Just so you know, that was your EPS session."

Conflict Resolution the Hard Way

In one of the company's locations, it became apparent that supervisors had avoided giving negative feedback to sidestep conflict. Specifically, the results of compliance tests had not been given to employees. These tests are a way of gauging whether individuals follow procedures correctly, and supervisors conduct them without informing employees. Nor, as it turned out, did they tell employees how they did on the tests, although the results were put in their files.

There were two problems with this behavior. One is that the tests are done partly for safety purposes. If the employees are not told the results, they don't know about any changes they must make in their day-to-day practices, which could endanger themselves or others. The second problem is that the supervisors, knowing who had failed the tests, formed negative impressions of those employees. They hesitated to give those employees positive feedback on their accomplishments, because of that hidden knowledge. It made for a punitive environment.

It all came spilling out with EPS. When employees questioned why they were not getting a better rating than they thought they deserved, they were told that they had failed the compliance tests. Justifiably, those employees were angry.

"If I wasn't doing it right, why didn't you tell me?"

The Supervisors' subterfuge revealed by EPS was a hard, but necessary, lesson.

Gaming the System

Spring brings mud as well as good things, so it wasn't totally unexpected that the HR team encountered some of it. Gradually, as EPS continued, it became apparent that some of the scorecards being sent to Head Office didn't mean anything. The actual EPS sessions with the employees had never been done. The scorecards being returned were just a tactic for reporting purposes.

There are always people in any organization who take pleasure in gaming the system. If a way can be found around a process, they'll discover it. There is now a post-EPS survey in place to check the quality and the impact of the session from the employees' points of view. You do, after all, get what you measure.

What Happened Here?

As EPS unfolded, the HR team could see its potential for having an impact on the company's bottom-line. It was there, not realized fully yet, but definitely there.

In June, 2004, one of the Central Division's locations had a productivity rate in inspecting trucks that was measured at a baseline of 200 per team, per shift. A goal of 225 was set, and over time that goal was met and exceeded, and then stalled at 240 in 2006. Suddenly, it was close to hitting 300.

The change was so sudden, the gain so high, that a visiting senior manager asked the supervisors in the location about it. What had changed? What new process was in place? He got blank looks, then an unexpected answer.

"The only thing that has changed here is the Employee Performance Scorecard."

Not even two weeks before the new goal was hit, EPS sessions had arrived at that location. For the first time, employees could see how their individual productivity rates compared to their group's average, and wanted to know what they could do differently. Supervisors asked employees who had high productivity to share their tips with their peers.

The teams were galvanized by knowing the goal and how well they were doing in comparison with it. Everyone at the site now knew the expectations, and all departments started to work together to support it. Some employees were going to their supervisors once a week to get an update on their productivity. It was the wise use of assets at its finest, all unleashed by EPS.

CHAPTER 18

SUCCESS STORIES

The first signs of spring had been a huge relief. They were proof that EPS had the potential to be instrumental in effecting further culture change within the company. At the same time, EPS was still fragile and in the rollout phase, and its full benefits were a long way down the road yet.

It was important to keep the momentum going in the right direction. The good buzz from employees and supervisors who had already completed the EPS process offered a place to start. That buzz could be shaped into peer testimonials, which could be inserted into the company's communication channels. Employees and supervisors yet to go through the new process could read about their colleagues' responses to EPS, which would help to demystify it, and make it real.

The second part of the communication plan got underway. Instead of providing information about the process, peer testimonials let employees know how it was actually working. Those responses made for a good story to tell as EPS continued to rollout over 2006.

Coming Soon

As EPS unfolded, some "trailers" were put in the company's Quarterly Results publication which goes to all employees. They would help to build a sense of anticipation for EPS, and keep readers informed of its progress. EPS was happening so quickly that the first issue for the year was missed, but the next three-quarters told the tale.

- Mid-way through the year, readers learned that 6,000 scorecards had already been produced. Eighty-five percent of employees had been rated as "skilled" or "outstanding" performers.
- In the third-quarter, over 15,000 had been completed.
- By the last quarter, almost 18,000 scorecards had been produced and over a thousand supervisors trained. About 90% of employees were earning "skilled" and "outstanding" designations.

Building the Supervisors' Confidence

During the training sessions for the supervisors, it became apparent that they had some hesitancy about their capacity to perform effectively in the EPS sessions. Many of them were open to the process and willing to try it, so it wasn't a matter of their belief in the possible value of EPS. It seemed more like they lacked confidence in themselves.

Part of the problem was that it was a new role for them, and it is not unusual for people to be somewhat apprehensive in such a situation. In particular, their concerns focused on that part of the EPS conversation which required them to elicit people's ideas for improvements in the work place, or to talk about employees' career interests. It wasn't what they talked about normally, and they were unsure how to manage it.

The supervisors got some reassurance from their colleagues who had already participated in EPS, when their peers' comments were published. Especially for those supervisors who were reluctant to buy into the process, the comments helped to make a dent in their resistance to change.

What the supervisors said:

- "It's an outstanding program. It helps to keep employees informed, makes them more a part of the team and helps them set priorities by knowing the importance of their roles."
- "I have a really good team and I think that overall it was nice for them to hear how they're doing. But it was also good for me, because you don't often get a chance to sit down and talk one-on-one."
- "A lot of people were glad we did it, and said it gave them a better understanding of where we are as a shop."
- "Sometimes, we get caught up in the hustle and bustle of daily operations, and we pinpoint things that don't happen right. But when you really look at it, 95% of things go right every day, and we're trying to recognize the positive things and the employees who make them happen."
- "It gives employees an idea of how we expect them to perform. It was important to explain why we were doing EPS, and relate how they contribute to the bottom-line of the company."
- "What I would like now is to be able to ask my employees to evaluate me as well."

Sharing Responses with Employees

The other important audience was the first-line employees. It had long been a good idea to stay away from supervisors, as most of the conversations they initiated were about problems. EPS was an entirely new experience, so it was important to insure that lots of their comments about the process got into print.

What the employees said:

- "I have worked here for 30 years and have never had a one-on-one review with my supervisors. It's about time, great stuff, extremely positive!"
- "I like the two-way feedback communication better than the one-way. I feel that I am being heard."
- "It felt pretty good to be told I was an outstanding performer."
- "What I like about the EPS process is that it lets you know what your supervisor thinks of your work. If everything is going well, you get recognition. And if things aren't going well, you get a chance to fix it."
- "This was a good discussion. Supervisors are changing. Previously, I always wanted to stay out of the Superintendent's office. Now, supervisors have the door open. When you ask for help and they tell you it will get fixed, it gets done."

Outstanding Performer Stories

About 15% of unionized employees received the rating of "Outstanding Performer." Their stories were shared with the whole company, and starting in 2006 over 100 of them were profiled in employee communications. Their stories reinforced the value of EPS, and gave the publications a strong human interest aspect.

The stories showed also how much in common the Outstanding Performers had. The stories contained certain themes, which would make interesting reading for all of those employees who now wanted to know what they had to do to receive the highest rating in EPS.

What the Outstanding Performers had in common:

- A passion for their work, and deep interest in it;
- Dedication to getting the job done;
- Persistence;
- A high level of responsiveness to immediate issues;
- A willingness to solve problems without delay;
- An emphasis on safety; and
- Able to work as a team player.

A Celebratory Message

In the third-quarter of 2006, it was time to tell people about the success of EPS.

"EPS was intended to push culture change further, deepen the engagement of employees in their work and give credit for good performance. It was designed to allow supervisors to have a one-on-one dialogue with their people, and encourage a two-way exchange of ideas and information.

Not all of the EPS sessions are finished yet, but the results to date are impressive. The vast majority of employees have been evaluated as being Skilled Performers and about 15 percent as Outstanding Performers. There have been a small percentage of employees identified as needing development, but from their feedback on the process, they believe that they know what they need to do to improve."

CHAPTER 19

PLAYING IT FORWARD

EPS was repeated in 2007, which gave HR a chance to consolidate it. At the end of the second year, there were few supervisors left who still believed that EPS was a one time thing which they could soon forget. Instead, it had become part of the way that the organization did things, and it had taken its place with other processes and systems within the company.

In 2008, efforts started in earnest to build further on EPS. In essence, what had been achieved so far with the process was that a platform had been created for the supervisors to have a conversation about performance with their people. With only a handful of exceptions, those conversations were taking place, and the performance reviews were being completed.

The next question to ponder was how well the supervisors could use the outcomes from that conversation to drive performance behavior in the right direction. It was the correct question to ask. The answer was that so far the supervisors seemed to be focused on completing a performance review, and not on leveraging its possibilities.

The team honed in on that answer, and started to plan the next evolution for EPS.

A Bottom-line Link

There is no point in having any organizational process in play which does not contribute in some way to the bottom-line. The company Business Principles are connected directly to the bottom-line, and all employees needed to use them to shape their thinking on a day-to-day basis. Maximum value from these principles couldn't be gained if only supervisors and managers applied them.

EPS, although still in its early stages, had a potential link to the bottom-line. It was a communication conduit that could provide a clear link between the Business Principles and real people doing real jobs. As the principles were used to frame the performance conversation, people were getting a clearer sense of what they were, and a sense of how they could contribute to them. These conversations were helping make the principles come alive in people's minds and cascading new thinking down into the organization.

HR was confident that supervisors were making more consistent use of the principles on a day-to-day basis, which was good for the business. There was not the same level of confidence that supervisors were explaining to their people how their decisions on a day-to-day basis reflected the principles. It seemed a better bet that what employees heard was the supervisors' end thinking in the form of direction or an order, minus the explanation.

It is those explanations from supervisors that help people gain knowledge and insight. That insight can change their approach to their jobs and improve results. Such coaching can't always be done on the spot. In real life, supervisors may not be available to give advice, especially in the company's case where employees and supervisors might not even be in the same location. EPS was a chance for some of that transfer of knowledge to get started.

To achieve the conditions for that transfer of bottom-line information, the next logical step with EPS was to make it not just a platform for a conversation about past performance, but one about future performance too. By looking at how their individual direct reports had done on each Business Principle, supervisors could determine where people needed help and coaching to perform better.

Enhanced Training in Coaching

Once the conclusion was reached that supervisors needed to coach their people to a greater degree, HR had to make sure that they could do it. It hadn't been that long ago that quite a few supervisors were surprised that coaching was part of their job. Given that surprise, it was pretty likely that they lacked good coaching skills.

In the U.S. Division, which had reached that conclusion much earlier than the rest of the organization, there was a coaching program in place already from CLG. This training was showing results. Next, it needed to be extended to the other divisions. The bonus was that the training could serve to reinforce the link with the ABC's program, and give participants a refresher on the basics that they were expected to demonstrate day-to-day.

Rating Protocol

The initial rating system of Outstanding Performer, Skilled Performer, or Needs Development/Too New to Rate had worked fairly well. It was a simple, clear way to differentiate people when the supervisory ranks were new to doing performance reviews with their people. As EPS deepened, however, some thought was given to how to improve upon it.

There were three issues with the rating system:

- Senior management didn't always agree with the rating outcomes from the field, and suspected that the Outstanding Performer designation was given too often;
- Supervisors needed more guidance on how to identify the correct rating for their people, and a protocol to follow that would simplify the task for them; and
- As part of the evolution of EPS, HR wanted to place more emphasis on the Needs Development category, which meant isolating this rating.

A new rating system was introduced, which would respond to the feedback and move EPS forward. It fit also with the belief that the supervisors were becoming comfortable with the practice of evaluating staff, and were capable of finer differentiation with people.

Five rating categories were put in place:

- Outstanding performer
- Superior performer
- Skilled performer
- Needs Improvement
- New

The final rating still depended on the numbers that are connected to an individual employee's performance in the work place. The big change was to include observations on some specific, critical behaviors that are known to be related to effective job performance. These critical behaviors were elicited from line management.

So now it can be noted, for example, that an individual is on time for work and puts in a full day. Supervisors can reward desired behaviors through recognition. They can bring undesired or less valuable ones to the attention of the employee in a systematic way through the EPS session and then follow-up with them. It is the ABC methodology in action.

Collected Employee Data

EPS provided an advantage that had been lacking before: a systematic way to collect performance data on all of the unionized employees in one place. HR reflected on how to make the best use of this treasure trove, and came up with a new, online tool for supervisors. It means that supervisors don't have to search through different systems, or perhaps take a wild guess, to know how their people are doing. They also won't forget what their people did in the beginning of the year, because all the documentation will be at their finger tips.

Instead, the new system displays, for example, attendance, compliance with rules, disciplinary actions, EPS' ratings and service date. Many supervisors, of course, have always been on top of how their people were performing. For some supervisors it has been more difficult, with their people in different geographical locations. The new system shrinks that distance.

It also offers a clear description of positive behaviors that support the Business Principles. This guide means that supervisors no longer have to guess which behaviors should be encouraged, and some consistency in rewarding the right behaviors can be achieved across the organization.

Two Handles on Performance

The new system gives two ways to approach ongoing performance: recognition for good performance and intervention for unacceptable performance. Every month, supervisors receive two reports: *Employees Who Meet Standards and Not Meeting Standards Employees*. Action is required on both reports.

- ***Employees Who Meet Standards***

This report lists employees who have met or exceeded key targets over the previous month. Supervisors are asked to select ten people from it, although there may be many more names on it, and make sure that they acknowledge the good performance in some manner. This recognition is *not* praise for getting on the list, but rather recognition for the specific behaviors the individual demonstrated that landed them on it.

Supervisors have lots of ways in which they can recognize good performance. It can be offered in a one-on-one conversation or in a team setting, or it can be through written communication. Whatever the method is that is selected; the key is to describe the desired behavior, and to offer the feedback as soon as possible.

This aspect of the new system is a significant change for both supervisors and employees. Attention is no longer directed only at employees who cause problems. Now, employees who go the extra mile can receive the recognition that their efforts deserve, which will help to reinforce their behavior.

There may be an element of surprise for some supervisors with this new requirement. It is quite possible that some of the names of people that may appear on the *Employees Who Meet Standards* list have gained a reputation for being "negative." They deserve recognition when they perform well, which may help some of the supervisors be less inclined to plaster labels on their people and see them in a more nuanced way.

- ***Not Meeting Standards Employees***

The second monthly report concerns those employees whose performance is in some way falling short of standards. Any employee on this list, and there may not be many, must be coached to improve the behavior that put them on it, and a written plan with detailed steps is required.

The members of this group are not being deemed as problems, but rather as opportunities. It is a chance for supervisors to be sure that standards and expectations are clear. Supervisors can be proactive in identifying gaps in performance. They can then put in place detailed coaching plans to help people be successful. It's a lot easier to change unwanted behavior when feedback and coaching is given to it promptly, than it is to let things go before that undesirable behavior becomes a habit.

Some new behaviors are anticipated through the new system. With employees who perform well, supervisors will learn to encourage that behavior through recognition. For employees who are struggling with performance, the new behavior that is demanded of the supervisor — insuring that coaching, tools and resources are the first-line of defense in dealing with performance issues — can help achieve more successful outcomes for employees.

And helping employees be successful is what EPS has really been all about from the start.

CHAPTER 20

WHAT WE LEARNED

On the face of it, EPS had been an impossible quest. There wasn't enough time to do it. The target audience neither knew about it nor wanted it. There wasn't any budget. There was no plan. There was not even a clear idea of how EPS would work on the ground.

In the beginning, it seemed like EPS was a failure waiting to happen. At the same time, failure was not an option. Now, it's another piece of culture change for the company. It, too, will serve as the foundation for future change.

The span between what seemed like failure waiting to happen, and EPS becoming a foundation for future change, yielded some lessons. Some lessons were easy, and some were hard. Some were new, and some were a confirmation of things known already. Most of all, it's now clear that the "impossible" can be done. The team even learned that the familiar customer service adage of "We do the difficult immediately, but the impossible takes longer", isn't true.

The impossible can be done, and done quickly. Even impossible change that was just a dream can be done.

Don't Assume

Just because people have the title of "supervisor" or "manager", don't assume that they are actually able to perform well in those roles. The person who graduates last in their medical class is called "doctor", but that doesn't mean you want to be that person's patient. You have to take a look at what managers are doing to know if they are competent and have all the skills and knowledge necessary to perform well. Their ideas about how to do the job may not be a good match with how the organization defines their role.

It was certainly true at the company. The supervisors thought their job was to get tasks done. The organization thought they were getting tasks done by working through people and managing their performance.

It's important not to assume that once training has been given, the way is clear for changed behavior. Graduates of training benefit from support and coaching to turn their newly acquired knowledge into on-the-ground skills. Even after the EPS training, it was noticeable that supervisors who had support from ABC coaches in the field were able to handle the new process more easily.

Reviews are Good for the Business

Most organizations do go through the messy, time-consuming process of setting annual business objectives. Once it's done, though, the process isn't over by any means. All of those objectives have to be divided up among the people who work for the company. Everyone needs to know what piece of the overall objectives will be within their role, and what they are responsible for achieving.

Everyone needs to be aligned across the organization if the objectives are to be met. Otherwise, they're just a semi-interesting set of words on a piece of paper, and it's pure chance whether or not they are tackled systematically. The best place to set objectives is in a performance review. The best way to track progress is through monitoring performance results over time and giving feedback on success and coaching on how to overcome barriers. It's the absolute bottom-line reason for doing reviews.

Hiding in Plain Sight

Part of performance reviews is putting a focus on development. How to help people build on and leverage their strengths is part of it, as well as how to tackle any new learning which is necessary for the person to function effectively. Improving competency has a direct contribution to the bottom-line for the organization. It's the short-term RIO on doing the reviews.

The longer term benefit is identifying which people in the organization have the potential to develop into the leaders the company will need in the future. Reviews allow these leadership candidates to be identified systematically. Without reviews, the people identified will likely be the favorites of their bosses, which may not be the best way to build for the future.

Perfect is the Enemy of the Good

Performance reviews normally start with setting objectives, then observing and measuring results over a stated time period. The company broke that protocol when it started with the actual reviews. It wasn't the "perfect" way to do it, but it worked. It got the process in place, and it helped to identify some underlying problems that needed to be surfaced.

EPS, like all projects, threw up a few roadblocks. The learning from them was that it's critical not to let them stop a project's momentum. If a roadblock is seen as an obstacle, everything stops. There are always going to be roadblocks, and conditions are rarely going to be ideal to introduce change. Equally, there is always a way to get something done. You just have to be open to finding it. Be flexible and find alternatives.

Sell Your Convictions

The HR team was convinced that EPS was a useful change, but not everyone else shared that conviction. Change can be hard and confusing for people, and given a choice, they often opt to avoid it. There was a great deal of time spent on selling the "Why" behind EPS to counteract this aversion to change. Every chance possible, people got to hear about the benefits that EPS might be able to deliver.

Change often threatens to take people out of their comfort zone. It means that people have to learn new thinking and skills. Even worse, they have to unlearn behaviors that made them successful in the past. So, along with selling the "why", the "how" had to be sold as well, so that people understood that they could manage the change.

While the "how" involved new learning, it wasn't as complicated as people imagined at first. Most of the supervisors had already learned ABC methodology, as well as the concepts of Q4 Leadership. That knowledge supported their efforts to master EPS. In turn, EPS can support other change in the future.

Real time feedback

A typical project in a large organization often takes two years, from the time it is on the drawing board to a pilot through implementation. Pilots get evaluated, and change can be made, but the sample size is small. Formal evaluation of the initiative doesn't happen usually until a year or two after implementation, when there is data to analyze. That time lapse can undermine new processes, as people lose their faith in them while they wait for the errors and gaps to be corrected that long finished pilots revealed.

With EPS, which went from idea to implementation in under a year, real time feedback was a great advantage. There was feedback from the pilots, which allowed the training to be tweaked. Because EPS was implemented division by division, the feedback from launch to launch could be utilized. This continuous feedback loop in a short space of time gave the chance to correct missteps early and to see gaps clearly.

There was, of course, a second advantage from the immediate feedback. The changes being made on the fly to EPS in response to feedback from the field gave the operations folks a sense of ownership over the project right from the start. They could see how their feedback was reflected in changes, not a few years down the road, but right away.

Stay Adaptable

When organizations implement new processes, the ideal is to be consistent and do it exactly the same way with everyone. Unfortunately, the ideal way to do it is all too often in conflict with reality.

EPS showed that it is better to build a process where "one expandable size fits all", than to insist that everyone is the same size. Want different measures? Okay, you'll have them. Existing systems don't fit with EPS? Okay, a different way will be found to create what's needed. Some supervisors can't do the sessions because of logistics? Okay, it can be done differently.

Connecting the Dots

In small organizations it can be a struggle to find ways to connect all the dots between big picture ideas and how things get done on the ground operationally to reflect those ideas. In any large organization, or even sometimes small ones, it's tough to connect the thinking at the top to the day-to-day behaviors of employees.

A lack of connection offers many opportunities for missteps. While none of them are deliberate, they still happen, and they can leave people gnashing their teeth in frustration. How do you connect hundreds or thousands of people so that they can move in concert?

EPS gave a sense of how meaningful that connection can be. For the first time, objectives were getting right down to the ground. Employees had a chance to see clearly the connection between what they did on a daily basis and the business plan. While it wasn't a perfect connection, it made a difference.

CHAPTER 21

TAMING THE BLUES

There is a compelling reason to do performance reviews. In an era where there are few destination employers left, and lifetime job tenure is doubtful, employees discover quickly that they need to steer their careers by themselves. Those steering efforts may not correspond well to an organization's needs if they prompt turnover.

When you listen to enough people explain why they leave jobs, you will hear certain consistent trends. The top reasons are: a lack of new learning and development; no visible career path into leadership; or, lastly, a poor manager.

Think of it as employees singing the blues. Employees may sing the blues while they are still in their jobs. Certainly, they're singing the blues when they vote with their feet and leave an organization. There's quite a cost involved with dissatisfied employees. Even if people stay or if they go, as long as they're singing the blues, there's not going to be much employee engagement or high performance happening.

"Sooner or later, everyone sits down to a banquet of consequences." These wise words were from Robert Louis Stevenson.

Every manager gets to choose whether the consequences with employees will be good or bad. Taming the performance review time blues is one place to start to push the odds to favourable consequences both for individuals and for an organization.

The Basic Reason

While performance reviews are only one tool that managers can use to engage employees, it is a critical one. The reason is that the skills that managers need to do performance reviews are exactly the same ones that they need to do their day-to-day work.

With just about any important task, managers have to be able to name and clarify objectives, and describe desired outcomes. They have to listen to their people, foster discussion and observe performance. They have to give feedback and coaching to reinforce good results and redirect ineffective ones. There is nothing different in doing a performance review, only it takes place on a formal basis.

There's a big problem when managers lack the skills to do performance reviews. They may need basic training in a process which is new to them to understand its mechanics. But if they lack the basic skills to do a performance review, they lack the skills to manage their business in general.

It All Adds Up

To achieve their objectives managers must decide how to divide the work among their available employees. Every one of their people has to do their share for the overall objectives to be reached. So it really is in the best interests of managers to pay attention to performance and support it actively.

Aligning everyone's objectives within work units doesn't seem to be clear to all managers, while with others it's crystal clear. Take sales managers, for example. They know that to reach their performance goals that they must stay on top of the sales representatives who work for them. They measure progress, recognize the reps who hit targets, and support and coach the ones who lag behind.

Maybe when it comes to how many miles of cable are strung, or invoices sent or trucks maintained, the relationship isn't as clear. The inexorable logic is still there, though. Unless everyone in a group delivers against objectives, managers' overall goals won't be met.

The Power of Consequences

Managers invest most of their communication time in giving direction. There is, however, a much better return on communication that is focused on the outcomes of performance. Feedback on performance is a very powerful consequence, and in behavioral terms, consequences are what really shape future behavior. Giving feedback has four times more power to shift behavior in the desired manner than giving direction does.

Managers in the company knew how to deal with poor performers, and were adept at applying negative consequences. What got overlooked was the need to focus on giving positive consequences to the overwhelming majority of employees who did their jobs effectively. EPS was a tool that highlighted this need and the power of consequences.

As a result of feedback, employees who had been given a "skilled" rating were demanding to know what they needed to do to get an "outstanding" rating. They began to share ideas. Good performers got better, because the right consequences were being applied.

Getting the Right Behaviors

In setting up a performance management system, it's not so much the employees that are a concern, but whether managers will use it or avoid it. There are some steps that an organization can take to help tame the blues.

Put Antecedents in Place

- Senior management plainly backs reviews, and keeps them on the priority list;
- Everyone knows their roles, and the targets set for the completion of EPS;
- Regular communications which remind managers of the timing of evaluations and their importance;
- Basic training for new managers;
- Refresher training for experienced managers as necessary;
- Specific training that supports individual managers' needs to do evaluations, such as training in coaching, conflict resolution or project management;
- Making the process simple and data easy to access; and
- As the time period in which evaluations will be done approaches, managers make it a highlighted item on every meeting agenda.

Put the Power of Consequences to Work

- Make 100 per cent completion of performance evaluations a business objective for each work unit, which makes it important to the person who runs it;

- Make completion of all evaluations for their direct reports a personal objective for every manager, which makes it important to the individual;
- Give recognition for progress generously; and
- Reward managers with positive consequences for making it happen.

Initially, rewards can be for just getting the evaluations done. Over time, an organization can choose to shape behavior by rewarding different aspects of the evaluation process. For example, it may be a completed, formal development plan that gets rewarded, if there is a general need for skills upgrading among employees to support overall business objectives. The key is to match the right consequence to the desired behavior.

When people get rewarded for their behavior, they tend to repeat it. You do want to make sure, however, that it is only desirable behavior that gets rewarded. Remember that letting managers get away with not doing evaluations without any consequences to them is a reward in itself, which will strengthen that undesirable behavior in the future.

Behavior Can Be Changed

EPS required behavior change. Initially, the supervisors' behavior underwent the biggest change. Instead of giving feedback pretty much only on undesired behavior, they gave recognition to the employees who performed well. As EPS continued to evolve, both feedback and coaching became more consistent. It was quite a distance in behavioral terms from where most of them started.

After their first EPS sessions, some of the unionized employees changed too. It wasn't a matter of working harder, for they already worked hard. It was a matter of being able to apply new knowledge about objectives and direct their efforts better. As well, being aware of how their performance was being evaluated, motivated quite a few of them to improve their ratings.

Once upon a time, many of the supervisors in the company believed that most unionized employees had little interest in their jobs or in the business. The employees only showed up for work so they could collect a pay cheque. Work was something that they did to fund the rest of their lives.

From the perception of the unionized employees, supervisors were the ones who yelled when mistakes were made, so it was best to avoid them if possible. It was best not to offer ideas or suggestions, because they would only be brushed aside. Better to keep your head down and just do your work.

EPS was a clear demonstration that it is possible to change behavior and perceptions. It was also a good example of how all behavior in the workplace is connected. When the supervisors shifted the direction of their behavior and gave positive consequences to employees, they got a positive response.

A Final Word

Was it worth it to do EPS? The story of it isn't finished, and it's still fragile. It's hard work taming the blues. There is one indicator of its value though. The company offers a stock purchase plan to all employees. Before EPS, the uptake from unionized employees was about 30 per cent. Then it went up to 70 per cent, which suggests that employees were experiencing a greater degree of commitment to the company and engagement with it. So, yes, it was worth it.

APPENDIX

Getting Started On Performance Evaluation

SETTING OBJECTIVES

The first step in performance evaluation begins with setting objectives for employees. This step involves some work and thought upfront on your part as a manager, and is a very important part of the review process. The key is to set objectives which are clear, meaningful and relevant to employees.

The First Step

The way to start is to ask two questions:

- What is the core purpose of this job?
- What are the critical outputs of this job?

To help with this task, you can examine job descriptions, which should set out the main tasks involved in the position. Most objectives will likely be set around these main tasks.

In some circumstances, objectives may be set that are based on an individual employee's needs. For example, there may be learning objectives if an employee requires training, either for a current job or an intended future job. Objectives also may be set around special projects to which an employee has been assigned. If you're to achieve certain behaviors in the work setting, such as team effectiveness, you might set an objective in that regard.

The Second Step

Once you've identified the critical outputs of the job, the second step is to put them in context with other factors that may be relevant in setting objectives. Consider how objectives will:

- Align with annual business goals for the company;
- Align with unit/department/team goals;
- Align with any company business principles; and,
- Align with long term goals.

The Third Step

At this point, you will have a preliminary set of objectives, which are relevant to the job, the individual and the company's needs. The third step involves "testing" them to be sure that you have identified the best ones for a particular job. Look at the objectives and then consider whether they are:

Specific: The more tightly defined an objective is, the easier it is to understand and the less room there is for differences in perception or disagreement about the specifics later at review time.

Measureable: Can the objectives be measured in a quantitative way and is there a reliable, objective source of measurement than can be accessed? How will the measurement data be collected? Is there a system which captures it, or do you or the individual employee have to record it?

Achievable: Given anticipated business conditions, are the objectives achievable? It's fine to set stretch objectives; it's not okay to set ones that only a miracle worker in absolutely ideal conditions can achieve.

Realistic: Is reaching the objectives under the control of the individual in the job? Does the employee have the skills and knowledge required and access to any necessary resources to reach the objectives? Then consider whether the number of objectives is realistic. Usually about five to seven objectives is a reasonable number, although this number may shift a bit depending upon the focus of the job. A very tightly focused job may have fewer objectives.

Time frame: Over what time frame can the objectives be reached? Will they be reached gradually over a whole year, or will some be done in a particular time period, such as a special project? If several of the objectives must be done within a certain time frame, such as an identified business quarter, are the objectives balanced across the year?

This "test" process will enable you to build a clear picture of whether the identified objectives are the correct ones. Most of the answers are "yes", "no", or "I can find out", which is fairly simple to do.

You may also want to think about how your direct reports' objectives align with the performance objectives set with you. Do their objectives add up in a way that suggests you will be able to deliver on your objectives? Are there any gaps?

At this point, you will have a list of possible objectives, subject to an agreement with the employees. The next step is to consider how the objectives will be measured.

DETERMINING MEASUREMENT METHODS

There are two parts to establishing measurements. The first is to decide how to measure an objective and what method can be used to access the data. The second part is identifying and describing the standards that will be used to evaluate outcomes.

Deciding What and How to Measure

In looking at the preliminary list of objectives that has been developed, a way has to be found to measure them. Sometimes, it's pretty simple to figure it out, especially when a job has specific outputs that can be measured. For example, if the job requires X number of units produced per hour, then statistics are likely to be kept on these production numbers.

Examine each objective and determine if there is a measurement system in place to capture the data. If there is none in existence, then you need to come up with a solution for gathering the data. How will the data be collected and recorded? Who will have responsibility for its collection? How often must it be done? What accuracy checks will be placed against its collection?

On objectives that can be hard to quantify, such as customer service, some thought needs to be given to how to measure outcomes. For example, with customer service, how would you measure successful outcomes? Calls answered within a certain time frame when a customer is on hold? Calls returned within 24 hours? Calls handled without the need to escalate them to a supervisor? Whatever the criteria you choose, you then need to determine how to collect the data.

Deciding on Standards

Once the specific type of measurement and its source has been identified, there is a further consideration. It involves thinking about your personal expectations for the individual and the job and the standards that you will apply in evaluating performance. While you may not be in the habit of expressing these expectations aloud, they will colour how you evaluate results.

You need to be prepared to describe to an employee not only what the measurement of an objective will be, but also you need to describe the standards that will be applied to evaluate that measurement and give it meaning.

For example, imagine that the objective is to send out customer invoices by the last day of the month, and the performance of this objective can be measured accurately through the company's system. When you look at the numbers, and see that 90% of the invoices have been completed and sent, what is your response? In your head, is the required standard 100% compliance, or is 90% a good output? What is the standard that you are using to measure results?

You need to identify these standards against all measurements, as they will be used to assign performance ratings to employees. What does an acceptable, good, better and best outcome look like? What is an unacceptable outcome? Do your standards change depending upon the experience and skills of an employee? For example, would you set a lower standard for someone who was new in a job? Are there any factors that would cause you to change your standards, such as a business downturn, an unexpected uptick in business volume or a lack of resources?

It is a manager's job to decide upon the required standards. The key is to be certain that the standards you will apply are reasonable and achievable, and that you are able to describe them clearly to employees.

It is useful to discuss performance standards with your peer group, so that the same standards are being used with related work units. When there is a common agreement on standards among managers, it is more likely that ratings will be consistent across groups.

THE EMPLOYEE DISCUSSION

The next step is to sit down with your employee and discuss the objectives you believe are relevant to the job, how progress will be measured and the standards that will be applied in evaluating outcomes. A way to make the discussion easier is to ask all employees to think about performance objectives for their jobs in advance of meeting with them.

It is a two-way discussion, as employees will have thoughts about what the main objectives of their jobs are and what good performance outcomes look like. The goal of the discussion is to gain agreement on objectives and desired performance outcomes. At the end of a successful discussion, both sides will have an identical and clear understanding of objectives and standards.

To reach this point of mutual agreement, you need to be sure that you head off any potential issues. What you don't want is for employees to leave the discussion with the belief that objectives have been imposed upon them.

Ask the Right Questions

Just as you asked yourself a series of questions in setting objectives, you can ask employees the similar ones and see how well your answers match.

"What do you consider the most important tasks in your job?"

"What objectives do you think are important to achieve in your job?

"What do you think is the best way to measure your progress to this objective?"

"How achievable do you think this objective is?"

"How reasonable is this objective for you in your job?"

"Are there any other objectives you think should be set for your job?"

You may get exactly the answers that match your thinking. You may get answers that you don't want to hear. Those answers are the ones that require the most attention. You can use effective listening techniques such as reflection or paraphrasing to probe gently around those answers to determine what the obstacle is in an employee's mind. The time to resolve any issues around objectives is before a new performance period starts, not after.

A Note of Caution

To prevent a discussion from descending into a debate, it's helpful not to start any questions with the word "why". When "why" frontloads a question, it is usually heard by the listener as hostility. It can put the listener on the defensive, which is the opposite of what you want to achieve in a performance discussion at any stage.

It's fairly easy to phrase questions to avoid "why." For example, if someone says "I don't think this objective is reasonable," avoid the natural reaction to come back with "Why do you think that?" Instead, a simple "Tell me more about how you see this objective," or "What do you see that could get in the way?" will give you a better understanding of what barriers the person perceives.

Your goal in the discussion is to have employees emerge from it with a clear understanding of what is expected of them, and to believe that they can achieve the challenges in their work.

Put It in Writing

Once you have reached agreement with employees about objectives, how they will be measured and what standards will be applied, put it in writing. It doesn't have to be an overly formal document, but it will serve as a common reference.

Remember, though, that there may be a need to revisit this informal document during the year. Business needs and challenges can change unexpectedly, which means that performance objectives may also change.

GIVING FEEDBACK

Feedback to employees is the most powerful tool that managers have to shape performance. Timely, accurate feedback lets people know when they are performing to expectations, increasing the chance that successful performance will be repeated. Quick feedback when performance is going in the wrong direction helps employees to improve their efforts.

Without feedback, employees have to guess whether their efforts are effective. In the absence of feedback, poor performance is actually reinforced and highly likely to be repeated. Good performance may not be sustained, because the absence of feedback often leads to behavior that diminishes gradually over time.

Being able to provide feedback is one of the most critical tools a manager can possess. Feedback is basically a conversation: it's easy to learn, and every day offers an opportunity to practice this skill.

The following guidelines will help you provide useful feedback to others.

Make Feedback Descriptive

- It's okay to say upfront that someone has done a "good job" as a way to begin feedback, but it is not sufficient to shape performance;
- Tell an employee what makes their performance effective — fill in with the actual details that you have observed; and,
- Emphasize the key behaviors that have led to successful performance outcomes in plain language.

Balance the Feedback

- Think through in advance how to balance positives and negatives in feedback, remembering that the negative will be heard distinctly, but not always understood fully;
- If the feedback is mostly positive, and there are no serious negatives, put any negative feedback in the middle of the discussion, which will "sandwich" it and have less impact; and,
- If there is serious negative feedback, place it toward the end of the discussion, but then follow with developmental suggestions and offers of assistance to keep it in perspective.

Be Direct with Feedback

- Managers are often tempted to soften negative feedback, which makes it much less likely that it can be understood accurately;
- Phrase negative feedback in a constructive way, and be plain and direct about performance issues;
- Listen to responses and watch body language to estimate how well the feedback is being received and give the employee time to absorb and understand the information;
- If resistance is encountered, speak at a slightly slower pace and in a lower tone of voice; and,
- Explain what the steps will be to support the individual in improving their performance.

Use Effective Listening Techniques

- Feedback may be clear to the speaker, but the listener may not hear it as clearly and accurately as you believe;
- Check periodically throughout the conversation that there is mutual understanding of the feedback; and,
- Wrap up the feedback session by asking the employee to join with you in summarizing the main points of the conversation and any next action steps.

Own the Feedback

- Only provide feedback based on your personal, direct observation of an employee's performance;
- Never take feedback from others at face value — either positive or negative, as you have no way of knowing how accurate it is, how the behavior was interpreted or misinterpreted, or whether it is second-hand or even third-hand; and,
- Be aware that blame-casting or scapegoating often comes disguised as "feedback" from others, and may come from multiple sources, without being the least bit accurate.

Feedback to Absolutely Avoid

- Feedback that is based on personality traits, i.e., do not suggest to an introverted employee that he or she needs to be more outgoing;
- Feedback that describes the employee as having an "attitude", as attitude, like beauty, exists only in the perception of the speaker;

- Feedback that is associated with gender, creed or ethnic identity; and,
- Feedback about any personal behavior of an employee when that behavior has no impact on performance in the job.

THROUGHOUT THE YEAR

Performance management is not a task that is done once a year, but rather throughout the year. You will need to track performance objectives and give feedback on progress on an ongoing basis. At the same time, many employees tend to put emphasis on the formal review, and there are some things you can do to prepare for it in advance throughout the year.

Note that some review periods may be shorter than one year. It may be appropriate to set a six month review for employees who are inexperienced, are in new jobs that require a steep learning curve, or have been given performance warnings.

- **Give Ongoing Feedback**

By the time a formal performance review arrives, employees should not be surprised by anything you have to say to them. If you've done it correctly, they already have heard the feedback in the course of their day-to-day interactions with you.

- **Keep Track**

When you give people feedback, make a note of it. Most work settings are busy, active places, with a lot going on at once. As a manager, you are likely to talk to people on the fly, and may not easily recall the details of such conversations that you will need at a later time for a performance review.

It's helpful to keep a record of notable behavior. It doesn't have to be a formal system, but one you can devise for yourself so that retrieving information is easier for you. A few rough notes jotted down will help you recall details later.

- **Stay in Balance**

Memory can be influenced by when an event happened. We tend to recall best what happens at the beginning of a measured period of time, and what happens at the end of it. What happens in between tends to get lost. As there are four quarters in a business year, and performance is happening across all of them, you want to make sure that you have a total picture of it for review time.

Another factor to consider in memory is that highly positive and highly negative events tend to be remembered better. Highly negative events are likely to have a greater impact in evaluating performance, and could make a review unbalanced. There is some research to suggest that a very negative event may require up to 16 positive events to counter it.

Look for Patterns

When it comes time to give feedback at a performance review, you will want to base it on an individual's usual or typical performance. Thus, in observing performance over a year, take note of the patterns that you see emerge in behavior. It is those behavioral patterns that will form the basis for most of the feedback that you will give. They may be positive or negative patterns, but they are repeated consistently, and are not one-off's.

There can be a secondary aspect to behavioral patterns. For example, you may observe that an employee is attentive to details most of the time, but under certain conditions, such as time pressures, seems to lose track of details. Rather than wait and spring this feedback on the employee during a performance review, give your feedback to the individual when you become aware of it to test how accurate your understanding is of the behavioral pattern.

Prior to the Review

- Close to the performance review time, collect and review all your observations and notes about each of your direct reports;
- Verify that you have solid measurements to rely on in determining if objectives have been reached;
- Evaluate performance against the standards that you established for each individual, which in turn will determine any ratings that you assign to an employee's performance;
- Keep in mind any unexpected events that occurred during the year that could have affected performance, but which were outside of any one individual's control before you assign a final rating;
- Give some thought to the development suggestions you wish to give to employees based on their performance and your understanding of where they wish to go in their careers;

- Ask your employees to prepare for the review in advance, and to come prepared to discuss their thoughts about their performance, what challenges they encountered during the year, their ideas about future development or job changes and what their thoughts are on the next year's objectives; and,
- Set the time and date for the review.